WOMEN OF SOUTHIE

Finding Resilience During
Whitey Bulger's Infamous Reign

PHYLLIS KARAS
WITH ANNA WEEKS

CHANGING LIVES PRESS

Published by
Changing Lives Press
www.changinglivespress.com

Library of Congress Cataloging in Publication data
is on file with the publisher.

ISBN-13: 978-0-99862-318-4

Printed & bound in the United States of America.

10   9   8   7   6   5   4   3   2   1

CONTENTS

1 Old Colony Projects

2 Castle Hill Park/Castle Island

3 Broadway Street

4 Saint Brigid Catholic Church

5 Saint Brigid Catholic School

6 Triple O's Lounge

7 St. Augustine's Church

8 St. Augustine's School

Black Falcon Ave

Reserve Channel

Reserved Channel

E 1st St   E 1st St

E 2nd St

E 3rd St

5

Marine Park

4 Broadway   E Broadway

E 4th St   E 4th St

CITY POINT

Swallow St

10

E 6th St

Shore Rd

William J Day Blvd

Sullivan's Castle Island

2

Fort Ir

Castle Island

Pleasure Bay

William J Day Blvd

E 7th St   Columbia Rd

William J Day Blvd

Head Island

each

Farragut Rd

SOUTH BOSTON – "SOUTHIE"

Loyalty is everything,
loyalty to family,
to friends,
to Southie.

From Phyllis:

To Chalese Renee Karas
and Amy Bowman Karas:
Strong beautiful women, devoted mothers,
loving wives, and adored daughters (in-law).

From Anna:

This book is dedicated to Kevin,
the love of my life, and our three miracle angels,
Julian, Maximilian, and Annabella.
We adore every precious curl
on each of your heads.

ACKNOWLEDGMENTS

To the strong and loving women in our own lives:

Phyllis Karas:

To my beloved mother, Belle Klasky, who taught me how to laugh and love

To my adored sister and best friend, Toby Bondy

To my remarkable nieces, Sheryl Perlow, Julie Hoffman, Beth Speciale, and Charissa & Madeline Bondy

To my loving sister (in law), Edna Karas

To my cherished friends, Sheila Braun, Merilyn Edelman, Barbara Ellerin, Karen Feldman, Ali Freedman, Barbara Gilefsky, Avis Goldstein, Arlene Leventhal, Karen Madorsky, Ellen Racz, Katharine Redmond, Hester Schepens, Barbara Schectman and Sarah Woolf.

And to my future, Belle May Karas, who took my heart the first time I saw her face.

Anna Weeks:

To my mother, Ethel Palazzolo, my everything

To my treasured sister, Christine

To my wonderful nieces, Maggi and Sophia

To my special cousin, Gail Moran, who has always been there for me

To my forever friend, Mary Devlin

To the team at Brigham and Women's who made my dreams come true, Dr. Antonio Gargiulo and Dr. Nicole Smith

To my prayer sisters, Dulce Cavahlo and Marie Ruff

And, of course, to two of the strongest women of them all: Francesca Minerva, our deeply appreciated publisher, who made it all happen, and Patricia Campisi, her right-hand woman every step of the way.

Without question, there have been men who have made their treasured marks on every aspect of our lives:

For Phyllis:

To my extraordinary sons, Adam and Joshua Karas, who stand beside their unparalleled wives, Amy and Chalese.

To Jason and Danny Karas, my awesome grandsons, whose parents lead them with love, kindness, and decency every day.

And to Jack, the wind behind my wings, because our sons were never raised by wolves.

For Anna:

To my beloved father, Salvaore Palazzolo, who will always live in my heart

FOREWORD

PHYLLIS KARAS

As a journalist and teacher of journalism, I seek out headlines that guide me to the stories I want to further investigate and write. For the small annex that sits south of Boston, affectionately called Southie by its residents, headlines abound. As Bill Gates once said, "Headlines, in a way, are what mislead you because bad news is a headline, and gradual improvement is not." This could not be more true when it comes to the reputation of the City of South Boston. A plethora of headlines offer a panoramic timeline of a city scathed by everything from famine to infamy, with adulations of its rich history, unique culture, and grand people few and far between. In this way, the world has been misled by the headlines, a few of which follow, and, dare I say, denied the opportunity to know a deeper story about a town firmly entrenched in its heritage.

GIRL WANTED—In a small private family—a young girl, 14 or 15 years old, either American or German, to take care of a young child. She must have good references. Wages $3 a month. No Irish need apply. Call at No. 89 McDougal-st.

An influx of Irish immigrants fled their Motherland to escape the Great Irish Famine of 1845–1849. Many of the 37,000 Irish Catholics who arrived in Boston settled in South Boston, turning Southie into a predominantly middle-to-lower working class, Irish Catholic community.

'WHITEY' BULGER SIDEKICK RECALLS BLOODY 1960S BOSTON GANG WAR

By the 1950s and 60s, Southie was no longer an "Irish Need Not Apply" town; however, it now faced the emergence of an Irish mob headed by James Whitey Bulger. As the undisputed and feared boss of the South Boston Irish Gang, he sold drugs and cracked down on those who questioned his gang's control of the expanding drug market in the city. While some Southie residents chose to view Whitey as a Robin Hood character who protected them from harder drugs and more corrupt criminals, others saw him and his mob as murderers and bullies, fearing his name and making certain never to cross his path. His reign inevitably came to an end when, after sixteen years on the run, twelve of which he spent on the FBI Most Wanted List, Bulger was captured in Santa Monica in 2011.

WHITEY BULGER, BOSTON GANGSTER FOUND RESPONSIBLE FOR 11 MURDERS, GETS LIFE IN PRISON.

It can be noted, however, that after Whitey had gone on the run in 1995, a rash of teen suicides hit Southie, leaving some residents to believe, perhaps rightly or wrongly, that Whitey and his incited "gang wars" had managed to keep the "bad" drugs out of their hometown.

DESPAIR TURNS INTO SUICIDE FOR SIX IN SOUTH BOSTON
70 teens hospitalized since January for trying or thinking of killing selves
August 17, 1997 by *NEW YORK TIMES*
NEWS SERVICE

Yet another headline, concerning drugs, nineteen years later in September 2016:

OPIOID OVERDOSES ON THE RISE IN SOUTH BOSTON

And then . . .

'IT WAS LIKE A WAR ZONE': BUSING IN BOSTON

Nearly a century after Irish immigrants of South Boston faced bigotry. Southie became the center of the now notorious busing scandal, which left the people of South Boston covered with an image of racism.

There is no description of Southie that could omit the infamous mark upon its soil, the Busing Crisis of the 1970s. This bad rap began with the court-ordered desegregation of its schools in 1974 when a federal judge, J. Arthur Garrity Jr., ordered white students from South Boston High School to be bused to the nearby town of Roxbury, which, in turn, would send its black students to South Boston schools. Southie erupted in fury, organized marches, and did whatever it could to halt the court order. Opposition to court-ordered school busing turned violent on the opening day of classes. School buses carrying black students were pelted with eggs, bricks, and bottles, and police in combat gear fought to control angry white protesters besieging the schools.

And finally . . .

CHURCH ALLOWED ABUSE BY PRIEST FOR YEARS

Aware of Geoghan record, archdiocese still shuttled him from parish to parish

Hundreds of church sex abuse victims continue to come forward

From a November 6, 2015 Boston Globe story about the Database of accused clergy in Boston Archdiocese: "Since 2011, at least 271 clergy—a mix of permanent and visiting priests, pastors, chaplains, deacons, religious order clerics, and nuns—have been publicly accused of child sex abuse in the Boston archdiocese. Accusations have led to criminal charges, lawsuits, and reviews by church officials. Priests have been convicted, sentenced to jail, and stripped of their religious duties. In some cases, they've been cleared by the courts and the church."

Despite the headlines that often exposed this insular community, keeping things out of Southie and its people "in" had been the nature of this community for generations. Thanks to its location, sitting directly to the south and east of downtown Boston, to which it is connected by a series of bridges, this densely populated neighborhood, with its present (and growing) population of 35,200, had a certain narrowness that formed, protected, and harmed its community in multiple ways.

But that isolation was inevitably destined to be destroyed. No location that hugged Boston Harbor, with thousands of feet of undeveloped property, could close the gates to these bridges and remain locked in the past. Gentrification began in the '90s and by 2002 was completely revived with young professionals, posh restaurants, and rents high enough to push out most home-grown "Old" Southie residents.

The "Old" Southie, during the 50s and 60s, had held the distinction of having more bars and churches per capita than any other city in the country. Here, as many residents proudly declared, you could drink and cavort all you wanted and walk a few feet from the bar to a nearby church and be absolved of all your sins. The men of Southie had their own reputation as loyal patriots with little fear of warfare, as evidenced by the fact that recruiters for the Marines were known to meet their quota in this one neighborhood. No decent Southie man would turn away from a good fight, either on the street or in the trenches.

Southie was equally remarkable for the fact that the first government-sponsored housing projects in the country were built there in 1940 as a cluster of twenty-two three-story brick buildings housing 873 low-income units. These projects offered affordable housing to those who qualified, creating close-knit neighborhoods, where parents felt their children were safe, and children found their days filled with playmates and friends. Neighbors became family, as mothers watched out for each other's children. These housing developments remained predominantly white until July 1988 when two black families moved into the Mary Ellen McCormack development.

Indeed things have changed drastically in South Boston as 10 million square feet of properties have been developed or redeveloped since 1996, making South Boston one of the most sought after places to live or do business in the state. The stunningly attractive Institute of Contemporary Art, the massive Seaport Square project, the popular Seaport World Trade Center, and the barrage of expensive and always packed restaurants along the South Boston waterfront are just a few of the vast changes that have shocked the spot of land between South Boston's two bridges.

But as the new residents began to pour in over the bridges, they were often unaware of the reputation for violence that did not come merely from the anger of busing, a reputation which had perhaps kept Southie out of tourism books. The historical and sensational facts about Southie, including busing and Whitey Bulger and the gang wars, the suicide and opioid crisis, the Catholic church scandal, and gentrification, fill hundreds, if not thousands, of books and newspaper and magazine articles, yet the story that is its best kept secret—the one that speaks of good and pure and real—revolves around many of the city's mothers and daughters, women of the "old" Southie.

In many ways, Southie itself has a matriarchal image, a city that loved its citizens and treated them kindly, while unknowingly making mistakes that caused collateral damage to its children. For it was the Irish women who came to this city in the 1800s, poor and hungry, who left their Motherland behind and formed a new one in Southie, who found ways to sustain their families with religion and food and hope and each other, who gave it its true character. And it was the descendants of these fighting women, the ones who inherited this Motherland, who stood up to what they considered the unfairness of busing 125 years later. And while the gangs that ruled the city were ruled by men, it was the women who continued to raise their families and protect their children and love their Southie and its men, the good and the bad men, the dangerous and the safe.

My introduction to this famous city began as I wrote the *NY Times* best seller, *Brutal: The Untold Story of My Life Inside Whitey Bulger's Irish Mob,* the memoir of Kevin Weeks, Whitey Bulger's chief lieutenant. Before I met the women of Southie, the main images I had of South Boston were of basements where victims of Bulger were murdered and buried, of bars, like Triple O's, where scenes of brutal fights and even murders took place yet witnesses never saw anything happening, of massive drug shipments of marijuana and cocaine that were distributed by Whitey's guys, of houses where extortion and punishment were meted out as frequently as beer and peanuts. Sure, I knew that Whitey's reign as head of the South Boston mob was now over, but the stories that had been related to me were still vivid and disturbing.

I understood that my vision of this city was woefully slanted and incomplete, but since I lived in a suburb fifteen miles north of South Boston, from which I drove to the classes I taught at Boston University School of Journalism in Boston's fashionable Fenway/Kenmore neighborhood, I only knew the nefarious nature of the mob. It was Kevin Weeks's wife, Anna, who introduced me to the softer side of Southie. Through her own personal and traumatic story and the stories of the women Anna subsequently introduced me to, I saw the world of Southie through a new lens. And there was so much more to learn from these women than from the headlines and stories that all too often turn Southie's women into uneducated, foul-mouthed caricatures of Abby Donovan, of *Ray Donovan* fame.

For starters, I heard only stories of survival. Of a city within a city. Of a very human struggle to keep it together while the rest of the country thought the people of Southie were imploding. Of contradictions. Of bad men who fathered lots of good babies. Of good daughters who fiercely loved their troubled mothers. Of addiction and physical abuse along with the possession of blind faith and the ability to forgive. Of adultery and jail time and profanity while dousing oneself in holy water in church multiple times a week. Of personal identity so strong it couldn't be defined by outsiders. Of acknowledgement of the difference between one bad hand and losing the whole game as long as you practice breaking the cycle. Of large and close knit families ruled by adored and powerful matriarchs who worked ceaselessly to keep their families respectable, strong, and attached to one another.

My education into the world of the Southie women continued when Anna and the women to whom she generously introduced me showed me what they considered "the real Southie." And it was most often a world where the violence of the streets of Southie, along with their own particular codes of loyalty, merged with the closely-knit neighborhoods they frequented. While they cherished living in neighborhoods where everyone knew their name and their families, insuring there would never be a reason to leave, there was, I soon sensed, also an underlying and undeniable sense of pain and trouble. These were not neat little lives, filled with calm and ease. While these women had little to fear from Whitey Bulger or the angry mothers opposing court-ordered desegregation, they met more than their share of violence on the streets of Southie on which they lived. Indeed, it was here, as well as in their own homes, that most of these women met deeply rooted problems that they struggled valiantly to overcome. Yes, neighbors looked out for other neighbors. And secrets were kept within each other's walls. But some of these secrets cried out to be shared and exposed. Some cries of help should not have been ignored.

When I began to contemplate writing about Anna and some other women of South Boston, my first thought was to write about women who loved bad men. But I soon learned the women Anna Weeks introduced me to were so much more interesting than any possible bad men in their lives. Some women were functioning and even more women thriving beneath a blanketed past of addiction, co-dependency, post-traumatic stress syndrome, domestic abuse, dysfunctional relationships, and violence, and yet still desperately loved the streets where they lived and felt gratitude for having lived there. Others were born into blessed circumstances of familial love yet bore witness to their neighbors' and relatives' own self-destruction. Could any of the problems that besieged some of these women have existed in another neighborhood or city or state? Of course. It wasn't the conflicts they encountered or the situations they were born into, but how they dug themselves out and their attitudes about where they've been: both hard and loving at the same time. Was Southie indeed a matriarchal figure to these women, nurturing and embracing each one, while imposing her own flaws and issues onto her daughters, crushing and harming them, holding them close yet pushing them away?

Loving a place where you or your loved ones may have suffered makes it all the more difficult to break out of one's cycle, or so I thought. As the details of their lives became clearer, each of these Southie women, I eventually realized, found the resiliency and strength, the bravery and the desperation, not only to put a pin in any destructive bubble that might have encased them or their loved ones but to become better women and better mother figures than in the past. These women had indeed made "slow progress," the kind of good news that doesn't make headlines.

I felt a budding admiration for the loyalty of these women and the belief that you should not turn your back on the trajectory of your life—good or bad. Over and over, they told me, each in her own separate and individual way, that Southie represented who they once were and always intend to be: flawed and faithful. There are obvious differences in the degree to which each of these six women lived their lives in Southie. Some inevitably faced more obstacles and pain than others. Some were "luckier " than others in various ways. But, as with most women, none traveled through her life unscathed.

The amazing thing is that these six women, the women you are about to meet, as they lived their lives, with inevitable crises and problems, somehow always knew this and even reconciled themselves to this reality. They were acutely aware that their city was more than its problems and that these problems would always be there, following them no matter where they lived. In so many ways isn't that what motherhood is? The undeniable bond that exists, whether you like it or not, to be born of someone or something that exists and marks you forever? Surely, the Irish mothers who adopted Southie as their new Motherland couldn't have known the power of such a bond with one's new city, with one's own place and role within it. Or maybe their own struggles taught them that survival is dependent on knowing who you are and to know who you are means never forgetting where you came from.

As a journalist, I found these women and their stories of loss, survival, struggle, acceptance, recovery, and growth relatable, so I set out to write it so others might find the same lessons and solace I have. Is it possible that there is a proverbial Southie that lives within us all? Don't we all experience and harbor some degree of shame, guilt, regret, remorse, and personal trauma? Don't all of our mistakes and problems make us flawed human beings while guiding our hearts toward an inner faith that we can move forward and become better? What would life be like if we were always living with our stigma and never our shining spirits? What if our "bad headlines" were all people remembered and all we allowed to accept about ourselves? Not only would that not be fair, it wouldn't even represent what's true.

The women of Southie, whom I have been honored to profile in this book, have taught me that bad headlines happen, in the news and in life, but should not be allowed to define us. Rather their lessons should enhance us, if we embrace and accept, not resist and hide. We are, as the following stories of the women of Southie prove, far more than merely bad headlines. And in that we can remember that we are more than what people think we are, much more than meets the eye, and in most cases, our personal truth, if we dig deep enough, can surprise even us.

1. IT'S NEVER TOO LATE TO LIVE

THE ANNA WEEKS STORY

"Once you grow up with the smell of the ocean in your nostrils, it is hard, if not impossible, to live far away from such a delicious scent." This is what Anna Weeks believes and remembers about her beloved hometown of South Boston, endearingly known as simply, Southie.

Don't let the humble moniker fool you. A separate island only reachable via seven bridges, Southie's remote access to Boston produced a culture that, while not exotic, would be considered enigmatically insular.

The culture, perpetuated by devout, loyal, and tight-knit people formed the city and informed the practices, beliefs, and physical aspects of its citizens. Anna was no different. It wasn't odd for families living in close proximity simultaneously gossiping about and protecting the myriad of secrets, many treacherous and dangerous, others inspirational and loving, that so many Southie families kept. One piece of gossip surrounded Anna's mother, Ethel Larsen, who stepped out of the bounds of her Norwegian heritage and married an Italian. Indeed by marrying Salvatore Palazzolo, from Boston's North End, Ethel broke the unwritten rule that Irish marry Irish and Italians marry Italians.

"I longed to be a Murphy, like my cousins who always fit right in," Anna says. "I had to work harder to be a true Southie girl, but I never stopped trying."

And neither did Ethel Palazzolo, who kept right up with the rules of being a Southie girl, not only to be the best dressed lady in the town, but to have the best dressed children. One of Anna's blessings of living and being raised in Southie, besides being paraded around in a brand-name stroller, was growing up in a three-decker house on Sixth Street near the beach and the 22-acre recreational park, Castle Island. On the second floor lived Ethel's sister, Rose and her husband Danny Murphy. The Murphys, unlike the Palazzolos, had the perfect last name for the neighborhood, plus they had the money to own the house.

Uncle Danny had the much-envied job of longshoreman, which meant he loaded and unloaded large ships that entered Southie's surrounding harbors. These were treasured jobs for you could not become a longshoreman unless you were born into the position and held a union card. This was the sixties and being a union man was a status symbol around Southie. Occasionally, when a container coming off a ship was damaged, the goods, unable to be sold at full price, might be distributed, though very quietly, among the workers. "I remember my mom and her two sisters being lavished with these rabbit fur coats that I thought made them look like movie stars," Anna says. "It was not unusual for all of my aunts to have the same silverware set or the same iron, great benefits from the docks. Sure, everyone pretty much knew this wasn't legal, but accepted it gratefully as just another one of the perks of having this desirable job."

As a fisherman, Anna's father, Salvatore, never made the kind of money his brother-in-law did. "But there was always enough money for my sister and me to attend school with our cousins at Saint Brigid Catholic school," Anna says.

Being a good Catholic was another "rule" of being a real Southie. While Anna didn't have the last name, she was able to check her religion off of the list. Anna's entire family was baptized, made first Holy Communion, and received the rest of their Sacraments at Saint Brigid Church.

"I will never forget the helpful instructions I got there," Anna says. "If dust blew into my eye during recess, I had to close my eye and make the sign of the cross over it. If I heard an ambulance, I was taught to make the sign of the cross over my forehead and say a silent prayer for everyone to be safe."

In her blue plaid pleated uniform, her starched white blouse underneath her navy blue cardigan, facing the crucifix in prayer, Anna spent her childhood comforted. In her world, which was a radius of blocks that connected her school to her church to her home and back again, Anna felt prepared for the rest of her life. "Or so I thought. If only everything could have been solved so easily."

What Anna would soon learn was that her obscure

beloved home had made quite a nation-wide stir, attracting much unwanted attention and earning a soiled
reputation. In 1974, the desegregation of Boston schools
stunned South Boston and other surrounding neighborhoods who were dead set against this new law which
enforced busing of black students into predominantly
white schools. South Boston schools were filled with
violence, their hallways lined with the Tactical Patrol
Force (TPF) as the Boston School Committee disobeyed
the orders from the state Board of Education. The media
turned busing into a racial event, depicting all of Southie's residents as racists, refusing to allow black children
into their white schools. Anna saw it much differently.
She and her friends, no matter where they lived, would be
bused across town, a town they never left. "The mothers
who were trying to prevent the buses from coming into
our town weren't bullies. They were just plain scared,"
Anna explains. "Whether you came from Charlestown,
Dorchester or Roxbury, these mothers saw no reason for
their child to board a bus across town only to be ridiculed
and not welcomed in an unfamiliar school."

The seventies were indeed trying times, as South
Boston students and families boycotted their schools.
Motorcades lined Southie's neighborhood streets, with
bullhorns sounding from block to block, yelling out,
"Hell, no, we won't go!" Anna wonders if a large part
of the problem about busing was protectiveness of their
secret paradise and the fear that the world would find out
about them.

Southie today, indeed, is a far different place than it

was when Anna was growing up. Some of the newer residents actually refer to it as Sobo (short for South Boston), rather than Southie or South Boston. Today, it reflects a waterfront playground that has been "found out," where people live paycheck to paycheck with roommates in exchange for a piece of the promenade pie.

When Anna was growing up, residents never lived in expensive condos. Those who were the most fortunate were able to own three-deckers, three-story homes that could house three separate families. Fifteen thousand of these three-deckers were originally constructed between 1880 and 1930. Those who owned a three-decker usually stuffed their family on one floor and rented out the two other floors. Each floor also contained a rear door connected to the porch at the back of the house. Windows on all four sides of each level allowed for maximum sunlight, while also providing little if any privacy from the closest neighboring three-decker home.

Those with low incomes, however, lived in the projects, first built in 1940 as a cluster of two three-story brick buildings housing 873 low-income units. Ambition to escape the projects was trumped by the desire to keep the closeness of those who took care of each other in these buildings. Most residents were lifers because living in the projects equated safety and happiness.

As if the uproar over busing didn't do enough harm to Southie's reputation, the sordid affairs of an influential family named Bulger would turn the city into a caricature of itself. First, William Bulger, a fierce opponent of busing, became its state senator, while his older brother,

James, "Whitey" Bulger, used his extraordinary power and charisma in the world of organized crime. One became the president of the Massachusetts senate; the other, the head of the South Boston Irish Mob. The Bulger history shared similarities with the illustrious Kennedys, in which Joseph P. Kennedy was rumored to have made his fortune in bootlegging, a good deal of which money went to the successful presidential campaign of his son John F. Kennedy.

"While most Americans believed in the office of the president of the United States, many in Southie turned to Mr. James Whitey Bulger, or 'Mr. Jimmy,' to get things done," Anna remembers. "The local consensus was that Mr. Jimmy kept the real bad people out of Southie, along with the bad drugs. He was our protector, there to support any of us 'ordinary folk' who might need a helping hand. I know there were many who insisted that he was pure evil and deserved no respect, that the only families he aided were those who had young daughters he could prey on. You either hated or worshiped him. I will always believe that, in some ways, the town was better with Mr. Jimmy and his associates. Without him, gentrification pushed families out of their homes, drugs like heroin soared, and family businesses could no longer afford to pay rent."

His womanizing was an accepted fact about Bulger's character, and he often preferred his harem young but street smart. He paid for many of them to attend private schools during busing and afterwards. One of those girls who could attract Whitey's attention was Anna's best friend, Brigid. "To imagine my childhood years without

Brigid is to visualize a blank board with no color or life," Anna says. "Even today, a good forty years since we met, I can still visualize Brigid's beautiful face the first time I saw her."

Girls Just Wanna Have Fun

It was in 1973 when Anna and Brigid became fast friends as third graders at St. Brigid. The girls also hung out with Tracy Killeen whose dad had been involved in a bloody gang war in Southie some years earlier, one involving Pat Nee, one of Whitey Bulger's associates and a substantial criminal in his own right. While the rest of the crowd languidly passed away the weekdays at their various schools, Brigid paid a lot of attention to her life in the fast lane. Despite the fact that she was still a teenager, she was socializing with guys much older than she was. But her most serious relationship was with Pat Nee. At the time, Brigid wasn't even eighteen.

Since Pat was close to twenty years her senior, Brigid's parents were understandably furious and begged for the relationship to end. "Ironically, since Pat was a father with children Brigid's age, I believe he understood the seriousness of this dilemma," Anna says. "But he couldn't seem to help himself. He was enthralled with her intelligence and her beauty."

Pat and Brigid shared a deep love for Ireland, its culture, and heritage, with Pat holding a strong allegiance to the IRA, which sought the collapse of the government of Northern Ireland. It hadn't taken long after their first encounter for the two of them to begin to live together in Southie for more than a decade. Although men like Pat had various girlfriends, they always stayed married to their wives and, like an old pro, Pat juggled his responsibilities at home with taking care of Brigid on the side.

"I couldn't help being jealous of Brigid's independence and her newfound wealth," Anna admits. "But while Pat always bragged about what a tiger Brigid was and how she could fight like a man, the two of them often went at it with such ferocity that I honestly believed they might kill each other. One night Brigid cracked the stem of the wine glass on the coffee table and stabbed him in the back. She told me, 'It was a fucking miracle we both got out of that one alive.'"

One night Pat and Brigid had invited Anna and her boyfriend Bobby to dinner in a Japanese restaurant in historic Faneuil Hall, along with Joe Murray and his girlfriend Sue. Faneuil Hall, with its indoor and outdoor restaurants and markets located right near the Boston waterfront was always a fun place to shop and dine. Plus, no one could overlook its historic significance as the place where Samuel Adams and other Patriots gave memorable speeches encouraging independence from Great Britain in the 1770s. Understandably, none of Anna's group's dinner discussion had to do with the War of Independence, but rather on Joe's taking Sue to the shooting range to work on her gun skills. A couple of years later, when Anna learned that Joe Murray had been shot to death by Sue, who was, by then, his wife, she couldn't help remembering how, during their dinner, Pat had told Joe he didn't think that was such a good idea. "I guess he was right," Anna says. "Sue never was charged with his murder, which she claimed was self-defense. Later on, I learned that Joe Murray had been selling marijuana big time in Charlestown. Thinking about that evening, I can see how I was always involving myself with these kinds of men. Even though I never had become romantically involved with these bad guys, I thoroughly enjoyed the fast life and the never-ending drama it brought."

Though Anna originally considered herself as an observer rather than a full-fledged participant in the bad-guy world, she saw how Brigid was always pushing things to the absolute limit. "For her, the more dangerous, the better," Anna says. "And she never worried about risking her freedom. Like so many of the people we hung around with in our hometown, she was no stranger to illegal activities. For her, that aspect made it all the more fun."

Eventually, Brigid and Pat broke up while still remaining friends. It had never been easy for Pat to juggle all his responsibilities to his wife and children, but he had tried. Anna and Brigid, of course, remained close friends and even moved into an apartment together. When they weren't working, they partied heavily. "Since Brigid had the little white car Pat had bought for her, we were free to go anywhere we wanted," Anna says. "That poor car was always getting smashed since we were lousy drivers, and, too often, drunk when driving."

Getting the alcohol and drugs they needed for their incessant partying had never been much of an issue. If they wanted to go to a local bar, they borrowed IDs from one of the older kids on the corner. "This behavior went along with the preconceived notion that everyone should drink and party at any cost," Anna says. "To us girls, as important as what and where we would drink was what we would wear. In truth, we Southie girls were, in more than one way, products of our environment. Much as our mothers had, we found it important to be in the limelight, to stand out in a crowd, to take great pride in our appearance. But no matter how old or young we were, or in what condition, religion still mattered to all of us. Despite how much we had been drinking or carrying on the night before, we made it to church, usually Saint Brigid, on Sunday. These values had been instilled in us from as far back as we could remember, and no matter how messed up our lives were, we were always praying the Rosary. Even until this day."

No matter where they went to party, no place had the charisma, the excitement, the downright authenticity of Triple O's, named for the three O'Neil brothers who owned the legendary bar frequented nightly by Whitey Bulger. "Lower Enders, the crowd that met at P and 6th as well as plenty from neighboring towns such as Dorchester and Charlestown, would pack this place," Anna says. "If there was an argument, cops were never involved. The fight was quickly taken to the streets where the bouncers would break it up, getting the problem makers, often bloodied and out of control, on their way. One night an actual murder took place at Triple O's but when the police arrived, everything was continuing as it normally did, with no one having heard or seen anything. It was part of the attitude that whatever happened in Triple O's stayed in Triple O's."

Since the bar was packed every night of the week, getting into Triple O's, no matter what you wore or where you were from was the first hurdle. With Brigid in their midst, Anna and her friends never had any problem passing that one. When patrons finally entered this darkly lit place, they could make out the long U-shaped bar on the right and the large, vibrantly hand-painted Disney cartoon figures and mirrors filling the walls, with Whitey himself often standing against a wall. Here he remained sort of hidden, never making himself obvious as he watched the crowd from the left side of the bar.

"Even inside the bar, there were huge lines to be faced, this time at the downstairs bathroom where girls would be reapplying make up, spraying their big hair, and many snorting lines of coke," Anna says.

When Anna and Brigid were there with Pat, they would get the special treatment, never paying for alcohol. "At the end of those nights, we would go upstairs and continue to drink until the wee hours," Anna says. "Understand that Whitey would never be involved with the coke. Anyone who used it would sneak off to do it, way too afraid to do any of that in front of him. Sure that made no sense since he sold drugs but cocaine was off limits here. At the end of the night, the lights would go on. Then you were able to see just how drunk and messed up everyone really was."

One night Anna witnessed what happened when anyone disobeyed that mandate. She was in the long line waiting to get into Triple O's, standing beside a friend who had a long and well-known history of using cocaine. Despite how hard Anna tried to get him to quiet down, her friend had been loud and argumentative, attracting way too much attention. When they finally got to the door, the bouncer took one look at Anna's friend and nodded to Whitey to come over. Whitey glanced at the guy and said, "Let her in, tell the other one to screw." Anna's friend suddenly turned quiet, then turned around and walked away without another word.

Getting cocaine was never very difficult. Some bought cocaine "off cuff," meaning they would pay later. Others would buy speed, also called Black Beauties, a combination of Amphetamine and Dextroamphetamine, while some preferred to smoke pot. "Charlestown kids often enjoyed Angel Dust, which was not that popular around Southie," Anna says. "However, there were some who did it, and you would hear crazy stories, about them feeling as if they were walking on air and they would act very strange. Some also took Mescaline, which could cause you to hallucinate. But, on the whole, the drug of choice at that time was speed and coke, because they allowed you to drink more and everything centered around drinking. So you would pack yourself into someone's living room, or sit around someone's kitchen table to post party after the house lights went off at Triple O's. Whatever it took, to keep the party going. We were so lucky. Our town was never boring from Thursday evening on." If it was Sunday morning, however, no matter your condition, you were off to pray.

"But that was all part of growing up in Southie," Anna says. "You drank, drove, and, if you were ever pulled over, you could usually talk your way out. Chances are the police officer knew your family or understood that Brigid was Pat's former girl."

And no matter what was going on between them, since Pat was so influential in the town, Brigid never missed an opportunity to throw his name around. "I occasionally did the same thing," Anna says. "When I was with Brigid, I never worried about the law, since I believed she could outsmart anyone wearing a uniform. Even when he was in prison, Pat looked after her. If she was in financial trouble, she would go to the Liquor Mart or Whitey or wherever Pat had given the word to give her whatever she needed."

But after a few years living with Brigid, Anna found new problems beginning to appear. She had blackouts, times she couldn't remember how she'd returned home. Unable to sustain any type of serious relationship, she always found herself heartbroken. "My life was a constant 'poor me,' a saying that eventually made sense in the halls of AA: 'Poor me, pour me a another drink'," Anna says. "And that was what I continued to do. Living with Brigid had increased our party time, as together, we drank and drugged and thought everything was a joke. So we laughed constantly, and when we were not laughing, we were sleeping, or still managing to work, Brigid at her waitressing jobs, me as an assistant for Head Start. Both of us were in total denial of our addictions."

Finally in 1992, after two years of sharing an apartment with Brigid, Anna could no longer deny that things were completely out of control for her with drinking and drugging. She moved out and joined AA and finally got sober. Brigid came to AA meetings with Anna, and during an eight-year period of sobriety, even put herself through the Laboure Nursing School at the Carney Hospital, where she graduated first in her class and was urged to enter medical school. "I followed her, yet again, this time to Laboure, enjoying the crucifixes and the Catholic atmosphere of the hospital," Anna says. "I took two classes, but after I got a D in anatomy and flunked physiology, I understood that this was not for me."

But, as Anna had always feared would happen, Brigid's demons eventually returned, and life got harder for her. "As our problems increased and our lives grew more complicated, we both understood that our friendship was doomed. We were heading in two different directions," Anna says.

By 2003, twenty years after they had met at the water fountain in Saint Brigid, Anna and Brigid had stopped seeing each other. It didn't happen all at once. "We knew too much about one another to simply disappear one day from each other's lives," Anna says. "So many moments only she and I shared, our own near brushes with death, the emergency rooms we visited together, one of us bleeding or in pain, me getting stitches after being smashed over the head with a phone receiver, the policeman questioning me about who did it, the two of us laughing at the officer until we collapsed on the floor. She was the best friend I could ever have hoped for, always in my corner, trying to make me see the light when I got involved in any bad relationships. She knew all my secrets, about my family, my codependency, my alcohol addiction, my poor choices in men, everything that made me the imperfect person that I was."

From Partner in Crime to Life Partner

Once Anna reached sobriety, the question was what was she going to do with her newfound life? Move out of South Boston where she had lived her whole life, get away from the people and places that had triggered her addictive personality? Try to combat her eating disorders so that she did not think she was fat every time she put a piece of food in her mouth? Concentrate on her compulsive shopping habits that often left her broke and unable to find a place to store all the clothes she bought? "None of the above," Anna says. "Instead, I did what any good addict would do: I found another addict to take care of."

And that wasn't hard. In 1985, at age twenty-one, less than a year after she got sober, Anna met the man who would change her life. Relating the story of their life together is painfully difficult for Anna. "He has been the reason I have always hesitated to tell my story," she says. "But there is no way I can eliminate the beautiful man who was my entire world for more than twenty years."

Referring to him only as "Michael," along with some other details to try and protect his privacy, Anna continues. "But the truth is that our life together was so filled with pain and joy, and despair and hope, with drugs and abuse, with love and dysfunction, that it can never be forgotten. Michael made me the person I am today, and while he nearly destroyed me, I accept the lion's share of the blame for our nightmare of a marriage. He was the sick one who struggled to become well. I was the well one who never accepted or understood his illness. All I did was love him so fiercely that I nearly killed the two of us. For now, this is my version and I share it with the hopes that other women may somehow find solace in its ending. I surely have."

For Anna, meeting Michael was basically love, or addiction, at first sight. She was a teacher at the Head Start program in South Boston and he had come to visit his cousin who worked there. Michael followed Anna out of the building, stopped her in front of a bank covered with mirrors, put his arm around her waist, and staring into the mirrors, said, "Don't we look good together?" And Anna looked back at the images and saw a tall twenty-one-year-old woman with rather large, brown, made-up eyes, overly long, dark blond, puffy hair, not a heavy lady but fearful that she was on her way to become one. The woman was dressed fashionably for 1985, wearing a knee-length plaid skirt and matching sweater over a long sleeved, white laundered blouse, navy knee socks, and brown penny loafers. The woman whose reflection she was staring at didn't know whether she should flee or stand still. But, in that mirror, she was standing beside an absolutely gorgeous tall man, in his early twenties, with dreamy blue eyes, hunky shoulders, and perfect posture. Thanks to his thick black hair, the definition of Black Irish.

When Michael asked for her phone number, Anna considered engraving it on his long elegant fingers. He called her later that night. "When we finished the conversation, I should have hung up the phone and never spoken to him again," she says. "But I did no such thing."

Michael, she now knew, was living in a halfway house getting support after getting sober. He was being tested weekly for drugs. He was armed with all the baggage Anna was struggling to rid herself of. Still, she began to excuse his history. What's a stint in prison and a drug problem? Big deal. All his minuses ironically added to his appeal. This was the norm in Southie.

"My friends weren't attracted to college guys," Anna explains. "We didn't spend our time at fraternity parties. Instead we traveled to prisons to visit the guys we cared about—brothers, uncles, ex-boyfriends, cousins, friends. The men we loved stole the jewelry they gave us, and we knew it. But that didn't bother us."

Michael tried to warn her, to tell her that she deserved more, that he could never be fixed, but she refused to let him go.

The two shared their sobriety stories, each of them understanding the pain and struggle the other endured. Like Anna, Michael loved fashion and jewelry and visiting the designer shops on Boston's exclusive Newbury Street , and she marveled at his exquisite taste for all the beautiful things neither of them could afford. "I reveled in every detail he offered me of his time in prison and halfway houses and treatment centers, certain that now that we were together, those days were behind him," Anna says.

Michael fit right into the South Boston "bad man" image Anna worshipped—so tough, so handsome, so cool. Like her uncle Danny who earned more than her fisherman father, Michael was a longshoreman, a profession she admired. Once she got him all fixed up, Anna was certain he would make tons of money down the docks, hauling crates off and on the ships that sailed in and out of South Boston's waterfront.

"Incredibly bright, Michael had a huge heart. I ached for what he had gone through as a kid in the late sixties diagnosed with ADHD but denied his meds by his abusive father, pushed to self-medicate," Anna says. "He particularly liked Valium, then coke. Though he had scary drunk blackouts, luckily he never did acquire a desire for heroin. Working with kids with ADHD, I understood his problem, and I knew I was the right one to help him."

In return, Michael was in her corner, encouraging her to further her education, even accompanying her to Cambridge College for her undergraduate courses and helping her with her papers and studies. When Michael was able to work, he made good money, too much of which went toward his drug habit, which included his drug of choice, Klonopin, used for panic or seizure disorders.

"He mixed the pills with booze," Anna says, "which made him nasty until he blacked out." Within a year or two of the relationship, Anna became, through her own fault as much as Michael's, she insists, an abused woman.

"Some abused women take too long to run out the door and stay there," Anna says. "And unlike me, they don't survive to tell their story."

She admits she was insanely jealous. Michael was so handsome and women were always attracted to him. No matter what he said to her, Anna could never understand why he had chosen her to be his girlfriend. "One night I came in and found him on the telephone," she says. "As soon as he hung up, I began to question him about who he'd been talking to. And I never believed him. As I pressed and nagged, Michael's eyes turned from their beautiful blue to an ominous gray, and he grabbed the phone and beat me over the head with it, splitting my head open. "

Anna didn't want to die that night, but she couldn't find the courage to shout and bring any neighbors to their door, so she stood there, letting him slam the phone against her head until the blood began to pour down her forehead and she thought she would pass out. "I could feel the power Michael had over me, and it made me weak and submissive and terrified," she says. "I was ashamed and afraid at the same time. No man had ever struck me like this before. This was a whole new world and I had no idea how I had ended up in it. Nor how I would survive this one night. But I must have caused it somehow, I kept thinking. It had to be my fault."

From then on, all Anna could care about was Michael's mood and what she had to do to make sure she wasn't rocking the boat. Her biggest fear was not that he would kill her, but that he would leave her. "I was more worried about what others might think than I was about getting killed. I had no choice but to drag my pathetic body to the emergency room, make up some stupid story about falling down a flight of stairs, and get my head stitched," Anna says. "It was a pattern that I repeated time and again, hating myself more than I hated Michael each time, fooling no one, not the nurses and doctors in the ER, or myself."

Michael had no problem making Anna believe the abuse was the fault of her big mouth or her insane jealousy. "But there were so many times when he was deeply ashamed of his behavior and the two of us cried in each other's arms," Anna says.

The wild roller coaster of love and hate lasted for more than fifteen years, most of which Michael had spent in prison for everything from driving under the influence, assault and battery on a police officer, usually when high and resisting arrest, shoplifting and attempted murder. With Michael in prison or detox most of the time, Anna was desperately lonely, and, like so many of the women she met in the prison visiting rooms, she had an affair.

All too soon, however, Anna realized that having this affair was the worst mistake of her life, even worse than being with Michael. And she cannot explain the fact that she didn't realize from the beginning that Anthony, the man she chose for this love affair, was a serious drug addict, one who covered it up well. "I thought he would bring me relief and peace, the total opposite of what Michael gave me," she says.

As Anthony began to use more angel dust, he became

even more dangerous. "This was such a powerful drug," Anna says. "It is basically formaldehyde, with long lasting effects. It gives you incredible strength while killing tons of brain cells. That was one drug Michael never touched. They used to say that angel dust was a Charlestown drug, that most people who smoked dust came from Charlestown. But Anthony was from Southie and loved dust."

After her father's death from cancer, unable to break off the affair, terrified of Michael finding out, Anna grew serious about killing herself. "I was so desperate and so filled with self-hatred that I couldn't find one reason to live," she says. "But when I thought of my poor mother, who was suffering so much from the loss of my dad, I couldn't add to her pain."

The affair with Anthony finally ended, though not before Michael did find out and came close, once again, to killing Anna. "I deserved everything that happened," Anna says. "I will never forgive myself for that giant mistake." In the midst of all this insanity, Anna began to insist she and Michael get married. "Every one of those sixteen years we'd been together might have been hellish, but I wanted someone to be with me forever," Anna explains. "But how could I ever have thought that person was Michael? He had just finished a lengthy prison sentence, he had a serious drug habit, and he had abused me over and over when he was high. But this was the man I wanted. And, somehow, it didn't seem that my life with Michael was all that unusual. Not in Southie anyhow."

Anna and Michael had spent barely six of those sixteen years in physical proximity of one another. The majority of the time, he was in prison, detoxes, shelters, and half-way houses. Still, Michael agreed to a ceremony at the town hall. Of course, nothing changed so, three months later, convinced that maybe a second marriage ceremony, a more lavish one, would link the two of them together in a new and healthy bond, Anna made the plans for yet a new start. This time, there would be a formal ceremony, complete with a designer DaVinci wedding gown for the determined bride, in the Catholic Chapel at South Boston's St. Augustine's chapel, the church with the oldest grave-yard in South Boston, followed by an elegant luncheon at Pier Four restaurant. Anna's sister Christine, who was the manager of an exclusive country club, struggling to mask her concern for her sister's impetuous plans, took care of all the details.

"This time my mother was more heartbroken and worried than before," Anna says. When Anna's mother pointed out that Michael cried during the ceremony, Anna's cousin Melissa couldn't control her anger. "He should cry," she said bitterly. "He's destroying her life." And, of course, once again, the wedding vows fixed nothing. Indeed, the Cape Cod honeymoon proved nearly fatal when Anna's husband became high and tried to throw her out of the car while she was driving them home.

As these months ran into more than twenty years, all the good years Anna had hoped to have enjoyed producing and raising a family, disappeared, leaving her alone, ashamed, dragging herself from one prison visiting room to the next, feeling as exhausted and confused and pathetic as she had been in the throes of her own drug and alcohol addictions. "I was still an addict. Addicted to the worst drug in the world, the love of an addict who could never be cured," Anna says.

Too many other times occurred for Anna to relate them all, though she has never been able to forget even one of them. "Some were not life threatening, but they still wore away at the fabric of my being, ripping the cover off the phony normal life I was struggling to exhibit."

Love Behind the Wall

Anna saw more of her husband in Massachusetts prisons than she did anywhere else. If Michael received a three or four year sentence, he was eligible for three visits per week. And Anna was there for every one of them. "All of us who entered the prison as visitors were doing time right along with our inmates."

Anna found every prison visit humiliating, no matter how she dressed or how well-spoken and polite she was. "I received the message early on that if I had a loved one behind the wall, I must be just as sick," she says. "This was the opposite of the message I received in Southie. There, it was perfectly acceptable to have a loved one serving time. It might even be rather questionable if you did not have at least one person you cared for currently in jail."

Yet no matter how humiliated she felt leaving prison, most of the time, Anna could not deny that she also felt like weights had been lifted from her heart and mind. Now, she would be able to sleep and stay safe while

Michael was away. Not in the arms of another woman, or attacking her in a drug induced rage, but securely locked in a jail cell.

Each time Michael was released, Anna knew it was a miracle that she remained alive until he was imprisoned again. One such morning as she was getting ready to go to work at Head Start, Michael came home early with a machete in his hand. Without thinking, she stretched out her hand to grab it from him. In seconds, her palm was sliced open. Grabbing a towel to wrap around her palm, along with her bag and keys, Anna managed to drive herself to the hospital, where they operated on her hand.

"By the time my sister arrived, I was prepped for the surgery, smiling like an idiot and talking about how clumsy I was to have done this to myself, grateful she would be there to take me home afterwards," Anna says.

This had become typical behavior for Anna, just the way it was for most abused women. "I would become tranquil and carry on, almost as if I had left my body and was floating around somewhere above the real Anna who was being abused down there," Anna says. "I had no time to feel sorry for myself. I needed to hold myself together so I could work both at my job and at getting Michael well. I always forgave him. It was myself I couldn't forgive for doing such a lousy job of fixing him."

When the panic attacks she'd had as a teenager returned, Anna needed her therapist's expertise more than ever before. Many of those earlier attacks had been so crippling that she'd found herself unable to move, so she'd taken Xanax to control the worst ones. "Now, because of my sobriety, I was reluctant to take Xanax again," Anna says. "I understood that the attacks were caused by oppression, by my not being able to speak my mind. I knew that if I kept all this locked up that a panic attack was the only way my body could release the fear and anxiety."

Anna's therapist tried to convince her she was capable of a healthy relationship, and would urge her to go to Al-Anon and AA meetings and to maintain a network of friends. He also recommended other therapists for Michael, whom he knew needed proper meds. To Anna, this therapist is one of the good guys and she will always be grateful to him for all he has done for her.

"I could fill far more pages with incidents in which Michael was out of control and I was scared to death," Anna says. "But why bother? This man whom I loved from the first day I saw him was an addict who grew sicker during our relationship, and he was acting the way addicts do. It is myself I have trouble excusing. Why I stayed is the question I will always be trying to answer. I loved him is the first answer. But it is not an adequate one. I stayed and allowed this horror to go on for twenty-seven years, sixteen of which we weren't even married. For that, I will never be able to excuse myself. It wasn't Michael who was hurting me. It was the addiction that he couldn't overcome. The rare times he wasn't high were evidence that my husband loved me and never wanted to harm me."

No matter what happened the night before, every morning in her classroom, Anna forced herself to be the best teacher possible for her students. "Carrying on with my daily business as I had been taught years earlier in Al-Anon, I simply had to look my best and move along," she says.

So Anna lived her double life, trying to stay upright on a dangerous merry-go-round she felt powerless to stop. If Michael were home, she was waiting for him to erupt. If he were in jail, she was waiting for a phone call or sitting on a prison bench. "This was my life," she says. "I learned to pretend that my life was good and normal, just like the lives of the teachers I worked with or the people I passed in the street. It was inevitable that some people knew what my real life was. Southie was a small town in so many ways. I knew I wasn't the only woman in town who was leading a double life. But no one would ever dare confront me, any more than I would confront another woman like me. So long as I dressed well, put on lots of make up to cover the bruises and kept my head high, then I was just fine. Nothing for anyone to worry about. It was a way of life for me, with the enabler becoming sicker than the addict. Al-Anon had taught me that you can have a life in spite of the craziness and that was what I just pretended to do."

After years of sitting by the door waiting for her husband to come home, Anna ultimately learned to go to bed by herself. She learned not to be crippled. She moved along and acted as if everything was fine. She taught school and attended college and took the necessary teachers' exams to be certified. She was a master of deception, coming close to deceiving even herself.

"The moment did finally arrive when I at least began to understand that I had no choice but to end our tortured relationship," Anna says. "For his sake more than mine. Most likely, I made his life and pain and addiction worse. I knew that I was also a prison for him and releasing him would be the best gift I could ever give my Michael."

Another One on the Prison Block

On November 17, 1999, Kevin Weeks, Anna's dear friend who had protected her so many times from Michael's rages, was arrested outside the three-decker brownstone that Anna and Michael shared with Kevin and one of his many girlfriends. Kevin's boss, infamous gangster Whitey Bulger, had been on the run since December 23, 1994, and had recently been placed on the FBI Most Wanted List. For a long while, Anna had been hearing Kevin muttering, "They're following me," but she'd never been sure exactly what Kevin did with Whitey. "Of course, I wasn't a complete nitwit," she says. "I knew he and Whitey did bad things. I preferred not to think about exactly what the 'bad things' were. I also knew he didn't have a regular job like I did. I knew lots of people like that, and I'd always figured they were either drug dealers, drug addicts, nuts on Social Security or government assistance, kept women, or well off. Obviously, I was not all that shocked when Kevin was arrested. I did feel sorry for his girlfriends, wife, and children. I knew what it meant not only for a person to be incarcerated, but for those who loved him."

After Kevin's arrest, Anna wrote him letters and he wrote back to her. And she tried to be home whenever he might call. "I happened to be on the phone with him when I was watching the removal of the victims' bodies from the burial site he had shown the authorities," Anna says. "It was the burial site where, fifteen years earlier, he'd buried them. Watching him in the news report on my television screen, as he stood there in his orange jumpsuit, I didn't know what to think. I couldn't connect the man who had played a part in the murder of these victims with the man who had been so good to me. I prayed for Kevin's forgiveness from God, begging God to stand next to him and not let him be alone."

While the nation viewed this horrific scene, Anna, sick at heart, still felt like Kevin needed protection. He needed his friends. She understood that Kevin was being accused of murder, and the murder of women, and it was ugly. But to her, he was a human being who had done bad things. "But I also knew that so many of us in Southie and maybe Charlestown as well, thought differently about criminals than the rest of the world," she says.

Many had little faith in the integrity of law enforcement. "My father put the idea in my head that you would never get rich working a legitimate job," she says. "And he had the experience, with some of the underworld Italian men, to prove his point. He'd gone legit when he became a married family man, but I'd been well schooled in my distrust for cops."

Like so many of her friends, Anna thought that if you were serving federal time, you just might have some smarts about you. Federal time meant a bank robbery or extortion, money laundering or drug trafficking. "Therefore, the general idea often went that if you committed a federal crime, you must be a little connected," Anna explains. "It wasn't a regular street crime. There needed to be thought and effort put into those types of crimes and these people weren't under the influence of drugs or alcohol. Smart criminals needed to ask themselves, 'Is the crime worth the amount of time I could receive?' You couldn't be a total idiot to figure out the answer to that question and make your decision accordingly."

Things did change regarding jail time after Whitey's gang was dismembered. Then, serving time, for many Southie people, could be looked upon as saving lives. "By then Southie had become so riddled with opiate addiction that some South Boston parents would do anything to have their offspring in the correctional system, the only way to avoid overdose," Anna says. "In jail, you didn't do drugs. Or, at least, that's what these parents hoped. Out on the streets, this opiate drug use had become an epidemic in South Boston and Charlestown. Drug users could only be detained for three to five days. Because of lack of funding for treatment facilities, these kids would wind up back on the streets to die. "

Anna remains convinced that the drug world grew more brazen when Whitey took off. "Whitey, the mastermind, knew how opiates like heroin would cripple a community and bring many to their knees," Anna says. "Maybe it was just coincidence, but I believe that if someone researched the increase in the number of deaths and crime, it would show up as a direct connection to addiction. These addicts would start with the opiates, with oxycodone, and graduate to injecting heroin, which was cheaper, and got into the system quicker."

Anna's father never bought into his daughter's being an alcoholic. He believed addiction stemmed from lack of will power, and if you drank when you knew you couldn't, you were weak. He used to say a little wine wouldn't hurt anyone, that it was good for you. Anna would say, "Dad, I can't drink period," but he would just shake his head unable to understand why.

When Kevin had been arrested, Anna's mother had been heartsick. She had always adored him, and when he went away, he would call her as often as he could. She had always felt more at ease knowing he had been looking out for Anna during all the drama with Michael, and she worried about his not being there for her daughter when her son-in-law returned from prison.

Living alone in her apartment after all the chaos and insanity she'd lived through there, Anna had no trouble keeping herself busy, working full time, taking four or five classes at a time and going to college full time all summer long to finish her degree. She visited Michael on every visit available, often went to Al-Anon and AA meetings, and saw her mother nearly every day. Each night, Anna would lie in bed, close her eyes, and picture the life she and Michael would resume when he got out.

Anna's delusion was interrupted when Michael did return home for brief stays. Without Kevin to defend her, she would hide out at her mother's house until Michael had either calmed down or was back in prison. "I hated myself even more," Anna says. "My therapist tried to make me see that I couldn't keep on lying to myself about our sham of a marriage, that Michael and I were slowly killing each other and the question was always who was going to be strong enough to say goodbye. But still I held onto my ludicrous dream."

Awakening to Life

In February 2005, Kevin was released from prison after serving less than six years, having pled out to his crimes and becoming a cooperating witness. The day he returned from prison he surprised Anna with a visit to her classroom. Soon after that, Anna's best friend Sarah convinced Anna to help decorate Kevin's new apartment in Quincy. From then on, Anna could not deny the strong attraction she was feeling. Sarah had no trouble noting the mutual attraction between her two friends, but Anna kept reminding her that she was married and on a lifelong mission to get Michael sober and have a real marriage. When Michael finally came home in June, Anna was relieved to put Kevin out of her mind and concentrate on making her marriage work. "But, to no one's surprise, not even mine, things never worked out the way I had stupidly dreamt they would," Anna says.

Not knowing where to turn, Anna somehow made the decision to move out of the brownstone and into her own apartment. As she found herself getting more attracted to Kevin, she knew she had to find a place of her own, one without memories of Michael, a place where she could at least try to put her tangled life in some semblance of order. "The minute I saw 43 Thomas Park in a historical area of Southie, I knew I had to live there," Anna says. "It was a clean, quiet and safe place, the perfect place to try and find some peace. The agent had to have known about my troubled marriage with Michael and maybe heard the rumors about my friendship with Kevin," Anna says. "I loved the feeling in Southie that we are all somehow one large and often dysfunctional family. There was no need for me to explain myself to her. She already knew plenty. It is also one of the things I hate about Southie, the feeling that there is no escaping the town, which often seems like this powerful person itself and knows everything, good and bad, there is to know about you. Whether it is a car mechanic, a teller at the bank, a bus driver or a hairdresser, they keep tabs on you and know more about you than you might like. Still I knew this was the way things went on in Southie and there was no other place I'd rather live."

Kevin thought Anna should consider moving into his apartment, but he understood her need to save face and not just move from the apartment she shared with her husband to the apartment of a different man. "I told myself that I would set up the apartment in Thomas Park as my own special place and stay there as long as necessary," Anna says. "That I would not jump into a relationship with Kevin. With every item I placed inside my new apartment, I felt as if I was proving my stability, my need to function as my own person, free of any potentially difficult relationships."

But with each trip to her new nest, Anna ached with the knowledge that what she was doing was also secretive and somehow wrong. "I just felt I could not spend a night in this beautiful place until I had let my husband know exactly what I was doing," she says. "I knew he would probably be relieved, but I still felt I was abandoning my husband when he most needed me. When I allowed myself to think that maybe I was young enough to start a new life, maybe even have a child, the voice in my head kept repeating, *You are a faithless Southie wife. You are abandoning the man who needs you. You are a loser.*"

It was the most difficult letter she had ever written, but Anna finally sat down and wrote Michael that she was moving out of their apartment, that she had paid the last few months' rent, and that he could have everything except for the personal items she had already taken. She didn't mention Kevin in the letter, but she knew that someone must have told him something about the two of them. She cried for hours, both as she wrote the letter, and after she'd left it in the apartment. There was no way of changing the facts that she was abandoning Michael and beginning a new relationship with another man. It didn't help Anna's feelings of guilt when she learned that several days after she'd left him the letter, Michael was back in jail.

As her attraction to Kevin grew, Anna had to come to terms with what he had done during his twenty-five years with Whitey. "It was one thing to love a drug addict with mental illness, and another thing to love an accessory to murder, and not just an accessory, but someone who had witnessed the murders, buried the bodies and then reburied them," Anna says. "Why would I want to get involved with a man who had committed such crimes? Yes, it hadn't been like he had killed the people with his own hands, but still, as an accessory, he was a murderer in the eyes of the law. Why couldn't I just say he was no good and walk away? Why did I see good in this bad man, a warmth and gentleness that I could not ignore?"

Still, despite her marriage to Michael, who she felt never qualified as a true gangster, Anna had sworn she would never get romantically involved with a gangster. "Criminals like Kevin might protect me, but I was never going to sleep with one of them," Anna says. "Sure, sometimes, I thought it might be nice to be taken care of like some of Kevin's former girlfriends. I could sleep late, exercise, drive a beautiful car, and have my own condo."

But she had always understood that if she acquired an education and a career, no one could take those from her. "I had lost Michael to addictions, to the arms of other women, to prison cells," Anna says. "I had lost other close friends to addictions. Now, I needed to acquire and keep anything that would bring me security, and Kevin was not one of those things. I kept telling Sarah I heard voices. One voice was whispering in my ear, 'He is better than what you have.'"

When Michael was arrested again, Anna made it clear that when he was released, she was going to give their marriage another chance. And Kevin agreed, insisting he didn't want to steal another man's wife and that she should do everything she could to make her marriage work. But if she needed him for anything, he would be there for her. Of course, the inevitable happened and Michael was released, but within days, he'd been re-arrested. A few hours later, she received a phone call from Michael. "I hadn't spoken with him in months and I was eager to hear his voice," Anna says. "I was still suffering from the pain of knowing that he had not even tried to look for me when I'd moved out of our apartment, that he hadn't answered my letters, that he hadn't cared one bit about where I had gone. But I went right down to Nashua Street Prison where he was being detained."

There, Anna and Michael sat, separated through glass and talked about the sadness that always surrounded them. Anna told him that she would help him in any way she could, filled with guilt that she hadn't managed to keep him safe. She left, aware how bad things looked for him then, that because of the Three-Strikes law of 1994, Michael could get life with no parole. If he did receive a life sentence, what would that mean for her? Would she have no choice but to find another life, to allow herself to begin a new life with Kevin? Or would she dedicate herself to visiting Michael, putting herself in prison for life as well? When Michael, however, received a six-year sentence, it did occur to Anna that if she were to divorce Michael while he was in prison, the only man with whom she could ever feel safe enough to start a new life was Kevin Weeks.

This was the first prison sentence during which Anna did not go regularly to visit Michael. In between visits, she sent him letters and cards. And the initial thoughts of a divorce, of making their separation final, arrived with its own set of guilt and pain. It was during his first year of that sentence when the two of them first began to talk about a divorce. Michael's cooperation only increased Anna's guilt.

Though Anna's relationship with Kevin was growing stronger, he never pressured her to hasten the divorce. Anna found herself reveling in his calmness, his strength, his love for his sons, his determination to build a new life free of crime. Life with Kevin was without drama. "He was grateful if I made him dinner, if I packed him a lunch for work, if I called him during my lunch break at school, for every little thing I did for him," Anna says. "Never had I enjoyed such a stress-free relationship or existence." *Still, what kind of a woman would divorce a man in prison?* Anna wondered. *Or marry a man who had pled out to five murders?* "A woman desperate for the love and companionship of a man who would never hurt her, who would never get drunk or strung out on drugs, who would protect her from anyone who might not approve of what she was doing to her husband in jail," Anna answered herself. "A woman who could not exist waiting for a man who had stopped loving and needing her years ago. They say when you put down the drink and drug, you put down the insanity. If and when I put down Michael, I was putting down the insanity. Such a simple lesson, but one so hard for me to learn."

Finally, in 2007, Anna gave up the pretense and the apartment in which she had spent less than a month, put all her precious antiques into storage and moved into Kevin's apartment. "My biggest problem was facing the world with the knowledge that I had left my crazed husband but was now in the arms of a murderer," she says.

Despite her inner turmoil, Anna knew she was doing the right thing. "I knew who Kevin was," she says. "And I knew, despite his past, that he had forsaken a life of crime, that he was a good man who would always treat me well and would offer me a calm loving life. I believed the pledge he repeated every morning that this day he would not commit another crime. His drama was in the past. We both believed we deserved better and were determined to give that to one another."

Anna's decision was helped by her mother's acceptance of her new life. "All she wanted was for me to be safe and happy, and she believed Kevin could make that happen," Anna says.

And, of course there was only one place where Anna wanted to live: South Boston. "I actually couldn't imagine living anywhere else," Anna says. "Sure, part of me was afraid because Kevin was living such a quiet life working and living in Quincy, ten miles away from Southie, and we had created this peaceful life where I could travel to the market without makeup or fear of running into someone unpleasant from our pasts."

Whenever Anna mentioned the possibility of moving back, most friends would say, "Are you crazy? Kevin can't be there. You don't want him back in trouble, do you?"

"Of course I didn't, but I needed to be there," Anna says. "Southie flows through my blood. The sirens and horns make my heart flutter. Nowhere else do I feel so alive, paying attention, yearning for more gossip. I desperately missed the smell of the sea, the familiar faces, stores and restaurants, the narrow streets, all of which had some special meaning."

Whenever Anna went back to Southie, she became paranoid, positive that people were following her, certain there would be hell to pay for what she had done to Michael. "Then I began to accept the fact I was not as important as I thought I was and that no one was all that interested in what I was doing or with whom I was living," Anna says. "Then, I knew for sure we would return to Southie, to the life I had always lived there. That didn't mean I was blind to the fact that Southie was a poor choice for Kevin and me. After all, I was still married to Michael, and Kevin would be taking a risk returning to the scene of his criminal life. Whitey was gone but who knew when someone might approach Kevin about taking over where Whitey had left off? I would also be heading back to the place where I'd done plenty of damage in my youthful years and then gone on to live a dangerous and painful life. One would think that was the one place I needed to escape from. But Southie was a magnet, good or bad, drawing us both back, literally, to the scene of the crime. And I, for one, was not strong enough to resist the dangerous temptation."

Kevin had no such worries. He had been out of prison for five years and had returned to Southie multiple times, actually for the first time within days of his release from prison. He feared no one. It didn't take long for Anna and Kevin to find a condo they adored. "And when I stood on the porch and realized I could hear the seagulls and smell the ocean, I was sold," Anna says. "I was back home."

Unfortunately, things weren't all that simple. When the owner of the condo, who had lived her entire life in Southie and raised her family there, decided having the infamous Kevin Weeks in the house in which she still lived was not a great idea. Kevin's face had been flashed all over national TV. Not only was he a convicted murderer, but he had even had a couple of run-ins with the owner's son. She could easily picture the bullets flying, maybe even landing in her living room "We were persona non grata," Anna says. "There would be no sale."

But Anna simply could not sit back and let this condo slip away. One morning, she wrote the owner an impassioned plea, baring her heart and soul to her.

"Dear Lucy," Anna wrote, "I just want to tell you how lovely your home is. I want to say that I know both your sons and your daughter, and have even spent time in your cottage up in New Hampshire. As SOON as I walked into the condo, I fell in love with it. Although I understand perfectly well why the names Kevin Weeks and Anna Palazzolo would alarm you, I AM by no way making excuses for either of us. Kevin has a SCARY reputation and my ex-husband has caused great harm around town. I can only say that today Kevin and I live a quiet life. Kevin works construction, and I teach school, and on my free time I spend time with my mom. I hope the people who purchase the condo love it as much as we did, right down to every glass knob. I thank you and your loving family again for allowing us to spend time in your beautiful condo. I wish you all well. God Bless You All."

Anna sealed it, and without telling anyone about it, mailed it.

Within twenty-four hours, the owner had reconsidered. The condo was theirs.

From that moment on, Anna was filled with a joy and gratefulness she had not experienced in years. Within three months, in March 2012, Kevin and Anna and her storage rooms and basements full of furniture and antiques and clothes were settled in their new South Boston home.

"After a long and painful journey, we had both come home," Anna says. Days after she and Kevin had moved into their condo, Anna went to the Cambridge courthouse where her divorce from Michael was granted on March 26, 2012. Michael, still in prison, waived his right to appear. "I could barely grasp the fact that we were divorced and I was living a life of calm and warmth and love with Kevin," Anna says. "This was the life I deserved and wanted."

When he was released, Michael went to a shelter. About two weeks later, he called Anna and said. "Anna, I just want you to know I made a safe return to society. I am well and want to thank you for everything you did for me."

That call just about broke Anna's heart again. "But then I looked at the man sleeping next to me and I was filled with the deepest love for him and a heartfelt gratitude that I was given this second chance," she says. "I loved that in my new life there would be no addiction. I would rather die by lethal injection than ever live with an active addict again. I was older now, and I knew I didn't have another run left in me."

Six months later, Kevin and Anna had their marriage

ceremony in their new home, the service conducted by a Justice of the Peace, a small dinner party for just a few friends and relatives. "That morning I went to church with Sarah and begged for God's blessings," Anna says. "I desperately needed Him to hear my prayers and understand what was in my heart. Incredibly, the readings on that particular Sunday were the same readings recited at my first wedding, and, to make the morning even more spiritual, the sermon was about marriage."

Anna listened to every word, sobbing softly, believing this was the message she needed to let her know her wedding was being blessed. She was certain that God was saying, "Anna, go and be happy. It's okay for you to marry Kevin. I will take care of Michael and ease your aching heart."

In Anna's serenity she found the screaming need to become a mother growing louder every day. She knew she was a strong woman who had endured far more struggles than the average forty-nine-year-old woman. And she was proud that she had managed to find a good and loving life at her "old age."

Anna understood only too well that at his age, six years older than she was, and a father of two sons of his own and a grandchild on the way, Kevin had no desire to start a new family. Yet when he saw how deeply his new wife wanted a child of their own, he could not deny her that dream. "We will make it work," he promised her.

No words could make her happier or more hopeful than those. "When I thought about what my body had sustained both from my early abuse and then from my marriage, I remained positive it could handle this latest hurdle," she says. "But I knew I needed even more help than my excellent fertility doctors. When I pathetically asked a nurse at the in vitro clinic during one of my morning blood checks if she could possibly pray with me, she led me into the bathroom where we joined hands and prayed for a miracle. She told me to believe that all things are possible through God, to go home and read about Abraham and Sarah in the Bible, to cleanse myself and prepare for a miracle. So I did. I read, I prayed, and I believed and continued to attend my adored rosary group."

Anna also found comfort during this stressful time from the pregnant Madonna statue at St. Anthony's shrine in downtown Boston. "I would take my shawl, roll it under my knees, kneel and pray the rosary before every Sunday Mass," Anna says. "I vowed to leave a dozen of roses for her each week, which I still do."

Indeed, the first attempt at a miracle occurred in April of 2014. Overwhelmed with joy, Kevin and Anna could not contain their blessed news. However, that dream came to a sad ending at seven weeks of pregnancy. "We lost our angel," Anna says. "To say that I was devastated would be an understatement. I can honestly say it was the worst night of my life. And that says a lot. Kevin and I were beside ourselves in grief, as I sat on the toilet and lost our angel."

When Anna approached Father White, insisting she was being punished since the beginning of the miscarriage had actually happened in church, he looked into her eyes and said, "Anna, God is not a punishing God. You are forgiven for all of your sins."

His words brought enormous relief. "I knew I had to carry on," Anna remembers. "Without sounding foolish, I have to say I felt as if I had been touched by God, that I had a spiritual reawakening. From then on, I re-dedicated my life to my faith."

When Anna and Kevin decided to pursue yet another round of fertility treatment, a most expensive decision, Anna had a feeling that the embryo was not as strong as the first one. And she was right. It did not take. "My disappointment was overwhelming," Anna says. "Because this time Kevin and I were out of funds. But it was Kevin who kept me believing we would be able to try again, that we could take out another loan. With that approval, feeling more confident and better educated with the process and stronger in my faith, we were off to the races again."

During this third round of IVF, Anna felt as if she was handling the fertility medicine with more ease. Indeed, this time, in the operating room, with Kevin beside her in identical surgical scrubs, their heads wrapped in surgical bonnets, Anna was prepared, holding onto her father's rosary beads, accompanied by a little statue of the Blessed Mother for company in the operating room.

Southie Baby

A true miracle occurred on November 3, 2015 at 12:38 p.m. when Julian Salvatore Weeks arrived, weighing six pounds, twelve ounces, nineteen inches long and absolutely perfect. "I was so emotional and grateful that the little living angel they placed on my chest was almost too much for my heart to take in," Anna says. "What did I ever do to deserve such a gift? My angel was perfect. His little cap of dark curly hair, his vivid coloring, his precious cries, and those huge blue eyes, just like his Daddy's, that seemed to look straight at and through me. All I could say to him was, 'I have waited for you my entire life.'

"I glanced up at Kevin, looking as handsome and proud as ever, the one man who had loved me with a strength I would never stop cherishing, as he used his gloved hands to guide Julian into the light, insisting he had to tug him to get him into this world. My heart swelled with joy for now I was complete. All the suffering and disappointments of my former life had disappeared."

The birth of Anna and Kevin's second child, Maximilian, on December 7, 2016, has unleashed even more love and joy than Anna ever imagined possible in her life. While she is aware that most people think she must be insane to undertake raising two children at age fifty-three, Anna gives little thought to what anyone else thinks. Nothing in her life has been conventional. Or easy. All that matters now is that she and Kevin made their decision together and are committed to making their new life together successful and joyous.

"I eat, sleep, and breathe my three boys, the loves of my life," Anna says. "And live by the sea in the only hometown I could ever love, Southie. I will never forget all the suffering and disappointments of my former life, nor will I ever stop being grateful for the gifts that have been given to Anna Palazzolo Weeks. Who would ever have thought such a miracle could happen?"

2. LOYALTY AT ALL COSTS

THE KAREN WEEKS RAKES STORY

Karen Weeks Rakes is no Southie cupcake. "I don't take shit from anybody," she says. Raised in a household where her father made brute force the daily staple of life, she learned at an early age to use her fists and to take no prisoners.

The girl who grew up in the Old Colony projects in Southie, living with a father who beat and humiliated her, who taught her how to protect herself from everyone, except him, and a mother who did far worse by never lifting a finger to protect her, has somehow managed to raised four terrific kids. Now fifty-eight, standing at a demure five foot, nine inches, with hazel eyes and silver hair that still turns heads, Karen is now married to Joe Rakes, a "good and decent man."

Karen's pedigree is as Southie as it gets. She's Kevin Weeks's younger sister, at least that was how the people of Southie referred to her. Kevin, the protégé of mobster Whitey Bulger was the most notorious of her family, despite Karen's two older brothers being Harvard grads and successful, law abiding citizens. She had a lot to live up to, and Karen's personality and choices resulted in her often being considered a female clone of her mobster brother. "But I never lived off Kevin's reputation," she says. "I didn't have to."

Bullied as a child herself, both in elementary school and in her own house, Karen despises bullies of any sort. "I had no safe haven," she says. "I wasn't a fighter back then so when I did start fighting back there was no stopping me. Ninety-seven percent of my fights as a kid were because I was defending someone in my family or a friend. I never went looking for a fight, but when it happened, I would be the one standing. I can't stand people who victimize others."

Karen never backed down from a fight, with either men or women. The words of her brutal father, "When you fight a woman, bite her tits," and "You beat them or I will beat you and you know which one will hurt more," still ring in her ears. "I liked to fight men by putting my father's face on them," she remembers. "Yet, when I came home from one of those fights, none of which I ever lost, I would show my dad my bloodied hand and ask him to fix my knuckle. He would pop it back into place. It didn't faze him one bit. My father was prouder of Kevin for working with Whitey than he was of my other two older brothers, Johnny and Billy, for going to Harvard. That was his mentality."

Home to the entire Weeks family with its three daughters and three sons was the Old Colony project, a 16.7 acre public housing project. Built in 1940 as a cluster of twenty-two-story brick buildings housing 873 low-income units, it is one of the Boston Housing Authority's oldest developments. The Weeks' apartment was about 1200 square feet, with four small bedrooms, a parlor, and a kitchen. The parents, John and Margaret, slept in one bedroom while the three sons shared a second bedroom. The oldest sister, Maureen, had her own bedroom and the two younger sisters, Patty and Karen, shared the fourth. As the youngest of the six siblings, all two years apart, Karen is convinced she suffered the most from hands of her cruel father who never hesitated to use his hands to slap or punch his children. "There were six of us," Karen says, "and each one of us would have a different story to tell about what he did to us. He was just an evil man."

Karen's sister Maureen whom she considered the "fair-haired child in the family," once told Karen there were "two daddy's, the bad daddy and the good daddy." But Karen says, "I never saw a tiny glimpse of the good daddy. When my sister Patty asked me if I remembered the day he slapped her, I said, 'Ask me if I remember a day when he didn't beat the shit out of me.'"

Margaret Donahue Weeks's parents, were, as Karen puts it, "Irish off the boat," while John Weeks's mother was English and his father Welsh and Irish. John grew up in the Bushwick neighborhood of Brooklyn, New York, while Margaret Donahue lived in Dorchester, a neighborhood bordering Southie.

John changed tires on eighteen-wheelers for a living and later worked for the Boston Housing Authority, bringing home, at the most, $160 a week. He had joined the army as an infantryman during World War II and was a professional middleweight boxer who'd also trained boxers. According to Kevin, a boxer, like his brothers trained by their father, John Weeks was "a throwback, a big puncher, the type of guy who would take two of your punches just to land one of his."

Margaret Weeks suffered from problems with her spine after a bad fall she had taken when she was sixteen. "It seemed every year she was in the hospital for some sort of surgery, like a spinal fusion or a knee replacement or for the joint pain in her knees," Karen says. "I have no memories of her without her crutches. The worst part of those crutches was that they were metal and if one of us dared to ask her for something in a store, she would crack you in the knees with them. That was my mother."

As was often the case, the neighbors in the projects knew each other's business, and most of the time, took care of their neighbors' kids as if they were kin. An Irish family of six children, such as the Weeks, was the norm at the Old Colony. When Karen was sixteen, one neighbor, Mr. McCormack, about the same age as her parents, was sitting in front of the apartment and told her to come over and talk to him. "He kept asking me if I was okay," Karen recalls. "And I said I was. He must have had a funny feeling something was wrong because he said, 'You know if anything is wrong, you can talk to me.' But I would never have done that. I knew I would be beaten if I told anyone what was going on so I never dared to say a word. My best friend Robin's mother was always so nice to me. 'You can come live here when you are eighteen,' she told me many times."

For all the years of her childhood, however, Karen found no possible way to get out of the house and away from a violent father who had rarely let her out of his sight. "Other kids had sleepovers and parties, but I could never go to any of them," she says. "I couldn't even sit outside with my friends. No matter how old I was, when he came home from work at four-thirty, my father would snap his fingers and that meant I had to get off the stoop and follow him home."

Every day when Karen was making her father's bed as she was ordered to do, she would stare at the .38-caliber gun underneath his pillow. The house had always contained guns and rifles, including two .22-caliber rifles in a corner of the bedroom. Even though the guns were never locked up, their father forbid them to touch them. Considering their father's violent temper, this was a rule no kid ever even thought of breaking. Karen, however, had no choice but to touch the .38 under his pillow, wondering each time she did what would happen if she used it to kill her father. "How badly I wanted to do it," Karen admits. "Jail didn't seem all that much worse than the house I lived in. But I guess I just never had the guts to do it."

The only decent thing with which Karen credits her father is spreading his love of books to all six of his children. Like her siblings, Karen is rarely without a book at her side. Two of her favorites have always been *A Tree Grows in Brooklyn* by Betty Smith and Truman Capote's *In Cold Blood*, though these days she favors autobiographies, along with crime writer Patricia Cornwell books.

There's no doubt that Karen, like her two brothers,

Billy and Johnny, who went to Harvard on full scholarships, and her other three siblings, has above average intelligence. While she attended South Boston High School in 1974-1975, during the first years of busing, there was far too little teaching taking place.

Karen has vivid memories of the busing situation in which Judge W. Arthur Garrity ordered a desegregation plan for Boston's schools, requiring 18,000 black and white students from South Boston and Roxbury to take buses to schools outside their neighborhoods. Since Karen's mother was on crutches all the time, there was no way she could take part in any of the dozens of Southie mothers' marches against this plan, and her father worked too many hours to participate in any other anti-busing events. Although Karen remained in South Boston High only for her sophomore year before transferring to Cardinal Cushing, she remembers how the state troopers were all lined up, both inside and outside the classrooms, making her wonder if she were in a school or a war zone. After a South Boston student, Michael Faith, was stabbed, school was closed for a month and metal detectors were installed, which forced students to stand in long lines before they were admitted into school.

"It was hard to do anything in a classroom when there were stateys (state policemen) all over the place," she says. "I had some black friends there but I couldn't ever understand why they wanted to bus kids, white and black, away from their own towns. My mother finally transferred me to Cardinal Cushing High because I wasn't learning anything."

There, Karen still managed to find reasons to get into fights, but one day she was called into the principal's office for an entirely different reason. When I heard my name over the loud speaker, I immediately thought, *What have I done now?"* she says. When Sister Mary Mulligan told her she was there because she had received the highest SAT scores of any student in the school, Karen was certain she was talking to the wrong person. But the principal insisted she knew exactly who Karen was and this was her score. Karen wasn't particularly impressed with this news. After graduating from Cushing, Karen enrolled in UMass Boston, but dropped out after one semester. "I just wanted to get out and have fun," she says.

Still, Karen struggles to remember the "fun" days that occasionally filled her childhood. "I think I worked hard to block out everything to do with those years," Karen says. "Sometimes a friend will remind me of something that happened when we were kids and I will say, 'Oh, yeah, like I don't remember.' I've been told the memory loss could be PTSD related. But then I will remember Christmas and how that was always a good day and we would all get everything we had asked for. One Christmas Eve, Johnny sneaked out and saw all the presents under the tree and teased us about what we were getting that he saw. After that, my father tied our doors shut with ropes and wouldn't open them until Christmas morning." When her father's favorite football team from his childhood in Brooklyn, the New York Giants, were on TV, the kids were again banned from the room. "He was certain we were all jinxes," Karen says.

Karen was grateful whenever her sister Maureen, who was a nurse and lived next door, asked her to babysit her daughter, one-year-old Angie. Maureen, like so many adults who had grown up in the projects, was pleased to find an apartment there for her own family. "I was just so happy to get out of that house for an evening while Maureen went to work," Karen says. "My friends would come over but I never dared to use the phone. My father would call and if the line was busy, I would be in trouble. My mother made sure to take whatever money Maureen paid me for herself."

Karen does hold onto the memory of some better times, like the years of step-dancing lessons at the Mary Madden School of Irish Dancing, certain even today she can still dazzle a viewer with her rapid fire steps. She laughs when she recalls the numbers she took at age fifteen, while babysitting for one family and the phone always ringing at home for her, her mother wondering why but her father, knowing she was taking bets on the street, just saying, "Let her get it."

Some of the fun Karen enjoyed on the rare nights she got out of her house was with a group of girls she hung around with in Charlestown. Charlestown, one of Boston's oldest neighborhoods, roughly five miles from South Boston, also celebrated a Townie identity among its close knot neighborhoods. Like Southie, Charlestown had a strong Irish population thanks to the migration of Irish during the Great Irish Famine of the 1840s. Though an intense sense of competition existed between the two Irish towns, in regard to their sports teams, both towns contained public housing projects and shared their negative views on busing. Today, Charlestown, like Southie, has felt the strong influx of new residents, and seen its populations of the very rich and the very poor even more pronounced.

"Mostly I hung with my sister-in-law, Peggy Cummings, and other friends. I didn't hang out with the Honeybees and Butterflies, who were one big gang in Charlestown," she explains. "You could easily tell the difference between the two groups. The Honey Bees dressed real nice, real feminine, while the Butterflies wore barracuda coats, tan jackets. When Southie girls wore those same jackets, they wore them inside out with plaid insides showing, with the collars up. Sometimes I hung around with my friends at Zito's bar in Boston, where we would have a few drinks and dance. Or fight."

Though Karen is the first to admit, "I am no Rebecca of Sunnybrook Farm," turning her back on any friend who needed her has never been something she could do easily. "I hung out with hard core friends," she says. "They were thick as thieves. The guys I hung out with in Charlestown were considered the bad guys, bank robbers, drug dealers, murderers. But they were my friends. I saw another side of these people. A side other people would never look for or see. And I knew they would all be there for me in a minute. They would take a bullet for me. We didn't trust outsiders very much. We relied on one another. People can label others by the crime they committed. I see a different side of these people. I don't know why, but it always seemed I was driving someone to prison. It was like I was the designated driver for visitors. I have a real problem with authority and hated to go inside to visit anyone there myself. But I sure knew how to drive to every prison in the state."

While Karen would enjoy drinks with her friends, she rarely found herself drunk. Alcoholism was not a factor in her house. Karen could almost excuse her father if he had been drunk when he beat his kids or did other awful things to them. But he did not drink. And he did not hit his wife. Karen remembers once when she was older and having a few drinks with her friends and her mother stuck her head out the window and said, "Your father always worried about you drinking," and Karen responded, " I should be an alcoholic with you two as parents."

The Great Escape

But most of any good times happened after Karen managed to get away from her father. That finally happened when eighteen-year-old Karen had had enough. "In the afternoon, my father sent Kevin out looking for me," Karen says. "I was out walking the dog, Becky, a pit bull. The only time I saw my father cry was when our other dog, Pee Wee, a black cocker spaniel, died. Kevin was a couple of years older than me and pretty much out of the house by then. But he was at the house that day and got sent to find me before he took off."

When Karen got home and her father hit her, she knew that was the last time he would ever touch her. "He went to work the next day and my mother went out, so I packed all my things and got a ride to Brandeis University right outside Boston to my friend Mary's dorm," Karen says "And I never went home to live with my father again."

The youngest of the six children in the Weeks household, Karen had already watched her five older siblings escape, leaving her the one who suffered the greatest at her father's brutality. "Boom, as soon as they were eighteen, they were all gone," she says. "But I had been the one left under my father's thumb, the one he would never let out of his sight. Even talking about him is like opening a can of worms." After her father suffered a stroke in 1984, he never called her Karen again. "He would call me the baby," she says. "He could barely speak at the end. He'd just mutter 'sumofabitch.' I had three kids by then and he'd been surprisingly good to them. Like my mother in her later years, just an old person trying to get into heaven."

When her father died five years later in 1989, Karen felt like a curse had been lifted. Until that day, she was still afraid of him. She had managed to write him a letter when he was still alive, telling him that even though he couldn't do what he used to do to her, she was still afraid of him. "I wrote that even though he had been sick and nowhere as strong as he used to be, I still saw him as the man who could just look at me and I would pee my pants," she says. "That's how deep my fear ran. He cried when he read the letter. My mother put it in his coffin."

It was only after her father died that Karen told her two older brothers what her father had done to her. "I was afraid if I told them while he was alive they would kill him and ruin their lives. I forget who found out first and told the other brothers. I talked to all three at different times but in a short period. They all felt the same way about him. I never went into details because why cause more anger and hurt? I don't think they ever talk about him anymore, like he never existed."

Finding a good man to trust and love after her nightmarish relationship with her own father would not be an easy accomplishment for Karen. One of the first men with whom Karen became involved was Poy, the father of her eldest child Michael. Poy, who owned a Chinese restaurant in Southie, was married and twelve years older than the eighteen-year-old Karen, who was working in his restaurant as a night manager, mostly taking orders over the phone, when they began their relationship in 1977. This relationship was to continue on and off for the next twenty years. "Poy was the first true love of my life," Karen says. "He didn't come much up to the house, but when he did, he called my mother 'godmother.' He often gave me food to bring home. He was very funny and people just liked being around him."

Karen was nineteen and had moved out of her house on Pilsudski Way when she found herself pregnant with Poy's child. "When Michael was born my mother said, 'Your father thought there was something going on between you two,' and I said, 'Yeah, you pimped me out for fried rice,'" Karen says. Poy, good looking with jet black hair, and at 5'4", shorter than the 5'9" Karen, never divorced his wife. Though he and Karen never married, Poy was a major part of her family, always attending family functions. "He has always been good to every one of us, especially to my girls and to Michael," Karen says.

It was Michael Kachuk, however, who married Karen, knowing the child she was carrying was not his. He became Michael's true father, in every sense of the word, raising Michael as if he were his son. "Big Michael was always there for Michael, bringing him to kindergarten, always keeping his eye out for Michael, loving him as much as Michael loved him," she says. Sadly, this marriage was not to last. Though Karen loved Michael, the two were young, just twenty when they married, and things didn't work out. Still they stayed friends until Michael died at age thirty-five, when little Michael was only thirteen. Karen will always feel a strong sense of gratitude to Michael for the loving father he was to her children.

Karen's relationship with Tom, the next man in her life, turned out to be a volatile one, punctuated with Tom spending time in jail and abusing Karen. Karen was pregnant with her daughter Taylor when he started to beat on her one night. "He'd been on dust that night and had tried to act like a hard guy," Karen says. "I covered my stomach to protect my baby. Afterwards, he locked me out of my house because he was afraid of what I would do to him. So I took Michael who was four years old and went to my sister Patty's and the next day Patty and I went back to my house. I waited on the stairs so he couldn't see me through the peephole. But I knew he would let Patty in. When he opened the door for her, I clocked him and grabbed a butcher's knife, pulled his head back, and was about to slice him from ear to ear. Patty kept screaming,

'Karen, stop! He's not worth it!' At that moment it certainly felt worth it, and then I remembered my kids."

But despite not wanting to risk losing her children, Karen still continued to get involved in brawls. "There were bar fights," she says, "when some asshole thought he was a tough guy. I couldn't stand when someone thought they could push around a woman. That's a coward to me. I had been through that growing up and in two relationships. Both times I turned the tables on these 'tough' guys. 'Surprise. How's it feel getting the shit beat out of you by a woman?' The tears of these grown derelict men were so validating, because I would just look at them and say, 'You're pathetic.'"

Sunday Morning Mayhem

Karen was up early one morning at her apartment in the Old Colony projects, checking on her good friend Jimmy while her three kids, Michael, eleven, Taylor, five, Jessica, four, slept soundly, as always, in her bed. Jimmy happened to be recuperating from a gunshot wound to the neck. From the couch where he lay, Jimmy remarked to Karen about the helicopters flying around the neighborhood. Something, they were both certain, was up. And then an incessant banging at the door jolted them both. "I went to the door and looked through the peephole," Karen remembers well. "All I could see was what looked like the top of a head, but opened it anyway."

The second Karen opened the door, a man, who had obviously been crouching down at the front door, his gun close to his side as if he were trying to hide it, rushed in, his clothes covered with blood. Jimmy sat up on the couch as he and Karen stared at the man, whom they quickly realized was their friend Mark Estes. "I could see that he was on something," Karen says. "All I could think of was that my three kids were at the end of the hallway, in my bedroom, hopefully still asleep and unaware of what was going on in our living room. Mark asked me to help him, knowing, I'm sure, that I would never rat out a friend to the police."

It took Karen little more than a minute to get Mark into another bedroom. The minute that door was closed, Karen ran to her own bedroom and woke her kids. "Guess what?" she greeted them, struggling to keep her own voice light and normal. "Nana just called and she's wants you to go upstairs. She's making you breakfast." Since Karen's mother lived just a floor above her and the kids always loved to go visit her and enjoy the treats she kept for them, there was no problem getting Michael, Taylor, and Jessica to head out in their pajamas to Nana's house. Karen never stopped being amazed at what a terrific grandmother her mother turned out to be. How a woman who had been such a pathetic failure as a mother had transformed herself into a loving grandmother was far beyond Karen's understanding. Maybe it was her future ticket to heaven, Karen guesses, one she wouldn't get any other way. But, at this moment, it was a blessing. She knew her mother would ask no questions, just be thrilled to have her three grandkids walking into her empty apartment, groggy but hungry.

As for how to deal with Mark, Karen was uncertain. She knew that she could never rat him out but she also knew she had to get him out of her house and make sure that the police didn't trace him to her. If that happened, she would be harboring a fugitive and could end up in prison, leaving her kids without a mother. Mark and his bloodied clothes were a serious problem and she knew she needed more help than Jimmy could provide to fix things. In his agitated state, Mark was barely able to explain that he'd been involved in a jewelry store heist and had shot his partner in crime, explaining the blood all over his clothes. But he had not killed him. Karen understood that the wounded man would seek revenge, a fact Mark surely also recognized. And she also understood that her own freedom would be at risk if the police found Mark now. Grateful that her kids were out of harm's way, she knew she would have to keep Mark here for at least a few more hours.

Karen called her friend Nancy, who had her own relationship with Mark, and told her, "You left your laundry over here." Nancy was quick to decrypt the message. Together, the two women sprayed the front of the door with Lysol to remove any traces of blood Mark might have left there and hoping it would get rid of any scents left for any possible police dogs to sniff out. Then they convinced Mark to put away his gun and get out of his clothes into a tee shirt and sweatpants that Karen found for him. "I raced the clothes up to my mother's washing machine, checked on my kids who, thank heavens, had no idea what was going on in their own house," she says. "I warned my mother again to keep her mouth shut, because I didn't want her to say anything to my sister Patty who worked for the cops. Then I went back downstairs and waited with Nancy and Jimmy for a good six hours until everything had died down."

Finally, Nancy pulled her car to the back of the building and got Mark out of Karen's house. But not before Karen told him that if he ever again came to her house with her kids inside, he was going to have to worry about a lot more than the police finding him. "I would have killed him if that happened again," Karen says. As it turned out, Mark was shot to death four years later. His murder was never solved.

"When I think about what could have happened that morning, I shake all over," Karen says. "The kids had no idea that Jimmy was recovering from a gunshot wound. They just thought he was sick. I always told my kids to learn from my mistakes, but this one could have killed them. Never would I open a door like that again. Yeah, I had made a decision not to rat out a friend. But at the risk of harming my kids? It wasn't a good decision. And I knew it."

Karen considers her loyalty to her friends immense, but not as unshakable as her loyalty to her four kids. What happened that traumatic Sunday, she is certain will never happen again. Nor will she let anyone else put her kids in harm's way. "I am a true Southie woman," she says proudly. "If you screw with one of my kids, you're good as dead."

Life with Whitey

Sometimes, Karen had a little help from her friends. When her oldest child Michael, who is part-Asian, was twelve, he was harassed by a local convenience store clerk. "The bus to Chinatown is across the street," the clerk had told Michael. Karen was literally ready to swing into action. "But the next day I get a phone call from my mother who knew how pissed I was, telling me not to leave work to take care of the matter; that it would be handled," she says. And handled it was.

As he walked home from school that day, Michael was met by his uncle Kevin Weeks and James Whitey Bulger, both of whom led him into the store to confront the man who had insulted him. After that brief meeting, Michael was never bothered again. Karen was not quite sure what happened but with Michael safe and happy, she didn't care to know any more.

But this was not the only time that mobster Whitey Bulger was a part of Karen's life. "When I worked at Whitey's liquor store, if I was stocking liquor he would smack me on the back to see if I would go off balance," she recalls. "It didn't work. Peripheral vision comes in handy. I think he smacked me just to see if I could take it. Sometimes he would just look at me. I used to call it the stare down. I would tell him he had the coldest eyes I had ever seen but I would stare back at him anyway. Even though he was my boss at the liquor store, I never feared him. The only man I ever feared was my father."

Sometimes Whitey would give her a ride home from

work. But more often he and her brother Kevin would come up to her apartment to watch the boxing matches on cable. It was during several of those visits that Whitey talked about Douglas, the son he had lost. "He loved that kid," Karen says. "It broke his heart when he died. Douglas was around six or seven when he passed away from Reye Syndrome (an extremely rare but serious illness that can affect the brain and the liver. It's most common in kids who are recovering from a viral infection). At the time they didn't know what it was. I never said a word. I just remember feeling so heartbroken for him. I couldn't imagine losing a child."

One night Whitey bought Karen a set of champagne flutes and a bottle of Dom Perignon champagne. Another time, he asked her to go to his house on Louisburg Square and wait for a phone delivery. When she saw the vast library in the house, Karen, an avid reader, was fascinated by what Whitey had curated. But it was Whitey's protection of Michael that impressed her the most. "I don't know why," she says. "But he was very good to my son."

However, Whitey's attitude toward Karen changed when she was pregnant with her second child "When Whitey found out I was pregnant with Taylor, he didn't think I could raise two kids on my own. Michael was five and I was single," Karen says. "He didn't think it was a good situation for me to be in. But I knew I could do it myself. When I refused to have the abortion he wanted me to have, he fired me from the liquor store. No one says no to Whitey and gets away with it. But he still kept an eye out for Michael."

Discussions about her mother are always painful. "She used a tape recorder when I was younger," Karen says. "She hid it so I never knew where it would be. But she would manage to tape a conversation in which I was disrespectful and play it for my father when he would come home. Like she would ask me to do something, and I might say, 'Give me a minute, Ma. I want to finish my homework.' But she would keep asking, always in a soft voice, until she got the answer she wanted, like my yelling, 'Stop bothering me. I'll do it in a minute.' My father had a job where he took orders from people all day long and he never came home in a good mood. The first thing my mother would do the minute he walked into the house would be to play the tape recorder. I believe it gave her pleasure to watch him give me a beating."

Karen says her mother's main priority was getting money for her weekly bingo game or to spend on yarn she used to make sweaters. "All my brothers sent her money," Karen says. "When Billy was first married, he wrote her a note that said, 'I had a little extra.' He kept doing that every month. One month when she didn't get the check, she called him, furious, asking, 'Where is my check?'"

At age eighteen, when Karen was working at the Chinese restaurant, she had done the same thing as her siblings, managing to save money to buy her mother a color TV. Having heard her mother always say, "Don't give me flowers when I'm dead. I want to see them when I'm alive," Karen went out and paid for a year's worth of flowers at Thorton's flower shop in Southie. That way, her mother would get a fresh bouquet every Friday for fifty-two weeks. "The only way to become my mother's favorite was to give her money," Karen says. "Money was the only thing that would make her happy."

Joe Changes Everything

Everything changed in Karen's life when she fell in love with Joe, including her on and off relationship with Poy, which then ended for good. Karen's husband, Joe Rakes, has his own Southie lore. On April 5, 1976, in the midst of the South Boston busing crisis, Joseph Rakes was the teenager photographed holding the American flag, aimed like a weapon at a black lawyer lying on the ground. It is this photograph that shocked the nation, earning photographer Stanley Forman a Pulitzer and Joe a two-year suspended sentence.

Karen is quick to point out that years later the authenticity of the photograph has been argued, with some indications that the white teen with the flag was, perhaps, just waving the flag with no intention of using the flagpole as a weapon to stab the black man. But the stigma of that emotionally charged scene, along with *The Soiling of Old Glory: The Story of a Photograph that Shocked America* by Louis P. Masur, the powerful book written about the busing controversy, has remained with the man whom Karen only knows as a hardworking, devoted husband and father.

For Joe Rakes, the entire busing situation had been far more personal than it had been for his future wife.

While his parents took part in ROAR (Restore Our Alienated Rights) and other anti-busing demonstrations, they removed Joe from South Boston High School and enrolled him in South Boston Heights Academy, an alternative school created during busing by the South Boston parents. Here, Judge Garrity's desegregation plan would have no effect. But that school transfer did not remove Joe from the danger on the streets of Southie. Fifteen years old and on his way to the Boys Club with some of his friends one afternoon, Joe was jumped by a pack of policemen from the Tactical Police Force who were supposed to be keeping the peace in Southie. Unlike the local police in Southie, the TPF had the reputation of going out of its way to beat up teenagers who even appeared to be heading for any sort of trouble. "I had to stay home a week to recover from the beating that day," Joe remembers. Whitey Bulger's criminal hold on the town appeared to have strengthened during that period, as some Southie residents felt a loyalty to the criminals to protect them, rather than to those who were sworn in to protect them.

Most days, Karen Weeks Rakes spends little time recalling that painful period in South Boston's past or the role of that photograph of her future husband in that historical event. She is just grateful that, after too many unsuccessful attempts, she has found love and peace and happiness with this good man. These prizes did not come easily.

A tattoo on Karen's right wrist reads *loyalty*. "Loyalty pretty much represents who I am," she explains. "I am, above all else, loyal to my family, to my friends. And especially to my husband, the number one person in my life. And no matter where I'm living, I'm loyal to Southie. I'm proud of being from the projects of Southie. There is no other place in the world where I would rather have grown up. That's what made me the person I am today. If Southie was the same as it was when I was growing up, I would never have moved out. But I'm glad I moved out when I did so my kids wouldn't have had to walk outside and see people shooting up. Everything has changed in the Old Colony neighborhood. They let people in without background checks so you never know who you're living next to. I lived there for forty years and never had those problems. But it is a different place now."

When Karen was living in those projects, despite her own painful childhood there, she managed to protect her own children, making sure they received the best possible education, clothes, confidence, and maternal love. "People have a misconception that if you come from the projects, then your apartment is a mess and your kids have crappy clothes and no manners," she says. "Well, my apartment was immaculate and my kids had designer clothes and are polite and grateful."

Karen's farewell to living in the Old Colony projects and South Boston revolved around Joe. Karen had known the Rakes family for years before she and Joe became romantically involved on February 9, 1996. Though the Rakes family had been living on Jenkins Street in Southie for years, when Joe's brother Stippo told his parents he was doubling their rent in 1982, they moved to Patterson

Street in the Old Colony projects, near where Karen's parents still lived. "After that incident when Stippo literally threw his parents out of their house, they never spoke to him again," Karen says. "Nancy would say that she had seven children but now she only had six. She told us to leave Stippo's name left out of her obituary."

When Nancy Rakes learned that Karen and Joe were dating, she put her hands on her hips and asked when they were getting married. Karen told her she and Joe had just started going out three months earlier, but Nancy said, "Aren't you two a little old for this dating shit?" Nancy Rakes couldn't have been happier when her son, age thirty-seven, married thirty-six-year-old Karen nine months later on Christmas Eve.

While Karen is proud of the time she spent at her job as a medical secretary at University Hospital in Boston, as well as later working in Maine with traumatic brain injury patients, her greatest pride relates to the impossibly good fortune that brought Joe into her and her children's lives.

When Joe found the perfect house for his new family in Kennebunk, Maine, 19 years ago, Karen did not hesitate. Though Kennebunk was the last place she imagined herself living, after looking at houses in Massachusetts, Joe convinced her to have an open mind as they took a ride to Kennebunk. "I told him he was nuts, that there was no way in hell I was going there," Karen says. "But when we went up there with a realtor the day of the May Day parade and the town was all decorated like something out of a Norman Rockwell scene, we found one house that was exactly what I wanted. I told Joe, 'If you buy this for me, I'll never ask for anything again.' He just said, 'Is this the one you want?' and that was it. It's a Cape, with a nice backyard, right down from the beach and in a beautiful neighborhood. A long way from where we started out."

Karen also considers herself blessed that her new life with Joe also included the woman who could show her what a loving and decent mother could be like. To Karen, Nancy Rakes epitomized everything good and important about a Southie woman and mother. "She was one tough Southie lady," Karen says. "And she was totally loyal to her kids. They might get into trouble, but she stood by them, telling them to hold their heads up high. She was a gorgeous woman, with red hair and beautiful blue eyes, a real sweetheart who would help anyone who needed her help. But she didn't take any shit from anyone. She could knock out any guy. Joe always said to watch out for her left hand. He was right. She had a vicious left hook. But Joe adored her. He would go down her house every morning and make sure she had her paper and her grocery shopping. When she loved you, you knew it. And I knew she loved me."

When Karen was pregnant with Katie, Nancy told her daughter-in-law she was going to have a real big baby. She was right. Katie weighed ten pounds, six ounces. "She adored Katie," Karen says. "And Katie looked just like her with strawberry blond hair and bright blue eyes." For Karen's birthday, Nancy always made sure her daughter-in-law got her favorite meal of steak and lobster. Nancy died of congestive heart failure in 2001, two days before Karen's birthday, but somehow she had managed to leave money for a steak and lobster dinner for Karen on her birthday. "I never had a mother who would even think of doing something like that for me," Karen says.

Karen will never forget one particular visit, after her father had died, to her own mother who was in a rehabilitation facility. "I was thinking about your father," Karen's mother blurted, while Karen was putting curlers in her mother's thinning hair. "He was a good husband and a good provider. He abused my kids, but he was good to me and that's all that matters."

Karen put down the comb and left. "If I hadn't walked out of that room, I would have choked her," Karen says. Later, at her mother's funeral. Karen did not cry. "I kneeled beside her casket and asked over and over, 'Ma, why did you hate me so much to have let him do so many awful things to me? What did I ever do to create such hate in you?' Somehow I had to learn to forgive her or I would not have been able to survive. The pain would have eaten me up alive. If she had been abused as a child, maybe I could have understood her a bit better, but she had always been pampered because of her physical problems."

Somehow, Karen has managed to forgive both her parents for the unbearable childhood they forced her to live. "It was a snake pit," Karen says. "But I had to forgive them, or else it would have eaten away at me."

3. NEVER LOSING FAITH

THE TORI DONLAN STORY

"I was a pain in the ass for most of my forty years," admits Tori Dolan, the freckle-faced redhead, who turns heads with her understated prettiness and swimmer's body. You wouldn't expect a fifth-generation Southie woman to look any less attractive. Especially a McGuire.

Tori is the second oldest of Elaine Sweeney McGuire's thirty-seven grandchildren, a high honor since Elaine is considered by some as the matriarch of Southie. Elaine lived her formative years in the Great Depression era and had taught all her children and grandchildren to be humble and appreciative of everything they had.

"Her presence was so huge in all our lives," remembers Tori. "She always walked with her shoulders straight, a strong presence physically as well as emotionally. Along with my grandfather, she raised ten children. They all became successful and strong adults and all admired her. She was such an example of love and decency. I could not bear to disappoint her."

Yet, sadly, Tori could not seem to help herself from doing exactly this. Especially when a string of suicides rocked Southie in the mid '90s. Six young men killed themselves while seventy teenagers were hospitalized for suicide attempts. "I was eighteen in 1995 when the suicides started," she says. "But I was fourteen when a close friend shot herself in her parents' bedroom with her father's gun. She was fourteen, too, someone I saw all the time. Her death rocked my world. I kept thinking of her poor parents. But even a few years earlier, I could understand wanting to kill yourself. I felt I understood why Jennifer had done it; the pain being so immense. And I was amazed at the amount of power she had to carry it through."

Tori was twenty when she slit her wrists. "No one was home at the time," Tori says. "I got into a tub and would definitely have died if my little sister hadn't forgotten her bus pass and come home and found me and called 911." Tori spent the next six weeks in a psych unit. Medicated most of the time, she was treated for anorexia and depression. She was safe there, which was obviously important, but her psychological problems were never helped.

When her serious suicide attempt failed, Tori considered it yet another thing she couldn't get right. But Tori is adamant that her own suicide was not a copycat version of the rash of suicides that were hitting Southie. "I had my own unique set of problems," Tori insists.

As a result of financial difficulties, her family had moved from South Boston to Canton, seventeen miles away, when she was in high school. "That was a tough move for me," Tori says. "In Southie there was this real townie feeling then, sort of like when the village raised the kids, not just the parents. Everyone knew everyone then and neighbors acted more like family than just neighbors. There was nothing I didn't like about growing up in Southie. Southie was my foundation. Even though I left it, I didn't really leave it. When people ask me where I am from, I always answer *Southie*."

No longer attending Catholic schools as she had before the move, Tori had become a student at the far larger Blue Hills Regional High School in Canton "When I'd been in high school and the depression would let up, I would dive into my schoolwork," Tori says. As a perfectionist, Tori had always worked hard to get good grades, even though that didn't come easy with her ADHD and the fact that her father was fighting colon cancer.

All Tori wanted was to make her father proud of her, so she'd put everything she could into her schoolwork. She set her sights high –to become valedictorian of the Class of '96, and she succeeded. Sadly, however, her father had died in 1995, almost a year earlier, so he never knew of her success. To Tori, despite her outstanding academic achievement, this was one more example of something she couldn't do right.

After her father's death, Tori had found herself unable to cope. "I was so perfectly broken at that time," she says. "My mother was devastated by the loss of the man she adored and equally broken, my little sister Ali needed guidance, and I was completely lost. My older sister Lanie was an overachiever and was on her own by then, doing so well in real estate. Watching how my mother was so lost without my father, unable to balance all our bills, Lanie kept saying she would never have a man to support her. My self esteem had never been lower or my social anxiety higher."

Things changed drastically for Tori when she was nineteen, living back in Southie, and had two wisdom teeth pulled. When the doctor gave her a Vicadin prescription, her boyfriend told her to tell the doctor Vicadin made her sick and get a new prescription for Percocet. "I did, and then I thought, Wow, this is so easy," Tori says.

Drugs from doctors' prescriptions continued to be an easy reach for her. "In our house, my mother had used them for her knee replacement. Now people I hung out with were easy for me to be with. I'm pretty intelligent, and I liked the good hustle of this lifestyle." With a big network of friends, both who bought and sold drugs, Tori felt successful and important when she could get drugs at a cheaper market price for all of her friends. It was as if she had scored a deal every time she could get Percocet easier and cheaper than anyone else. "I'd been experimenting with some drugs when I was seventeen, but now at nineteen, I was a daily user. I was a heroin addict," she admits. Waiting for a dealer was a lot faster than standing in line trying to get into a club or bar. By 1997, when she was twenty and had her own failed suicide attempt, Tori found the streets of South Boston infested with Oxycontin. "I continued to work the system," she says. "Drugs weren't as controlled when Oxycontin hit the street. But six or seven years later, people were dying of heroin here. It was a matter of picking your poison. It was insidious but subtle. Now you are suffering and the drugs are controlling you completely. I stopped hanging with people if they weren't using drugs and hung only with those who were doing what I was doing."

Tori understood only too well that what she was doing was going against everything she had been taught as a kid. Her entire family was well respected in Southie and that set a bar and a precedent for how she was expected to act. "My mother always said that when you step out of the door, you represent your family," Tori explained. "If you have an issue with your family, you don't talk to outsiders about it. You don't shit where you eat. You don't run amok in your neighborhood. You take pride in your neighborhood. Yet, look at what I was doing. There were no excuses."

Tori believes that the drug scene in South Boston had changed after Whitey Bulger, the head of the South Boston Irish Mob, had gone on the run in 1994. "When he was around, you could get the stuff, but Whitey didn't let it get out of hand," Tori says. "People who sold the drugs on the street had to pay taxes to Whitey so it wasn't a free-for-all. He monitored the stuff and he wasn't letting shit on the market because it was his nephews or his friends' kids who were using and he didn't want them dying. When he took off, it was an absolute shit show with the stuff on the streets."

From Speed to Acceleration

Everything in her life finally changed one afternoon in 2002 when Tori was twenty-five. She was lying on her younger sister's bed, watching television and waiting for her dealer to call her back. "I knew nothing about the military," she says, "but this commercial came on called 'Accelerate Your Life' about the Navy. It gave a number to call and I made the call. All I knew was that I didn't have ten cents to my name, nor a job, and I had to get out of Southie. I was longing for structure and discipline because I was a hot mess. All I wanted was a ticket out of Dodge."

Ten minutes later, her drug dealer had arrived with her drugs, and ten minutes after that, the local recruiter was at her house. "I hadn't realized that these recruiters were paid by commission," Tori says. "Obviously, he saw I was a female and then he asked me three questions. Did I have a criminal record, was I over eighteen, and was I willing to leave ASAP?"

Tori answered no to the first question and yes to the next two. She had met the criteria. The fact that she had graduated with highest honors from high school and had even gone to college at UMass Boston for a year made her stand out even more. Never before had Tori even thought about being in the military, nor had anyone in her family ever been in the military. "The recruiter wasn't concerned that I was now high as a kite, so he took me to a local office on Summer Street where I took a standardized test," Tori says. She needed a 31 to get in but even though, or perhaps because, she was high on heroin she got an 89. With such a high score it was suggested Tori apply for officer training, but she told the recruiter she wanted to be a medic.

The next morning the recruiter met Tori to take her for her drug test, which she told him she could not pass. "That whole decade is kind of blurry to me," Tori says, "but I do remember we went to a vitamin store on Hancock Street in Quincy where he bought stuff, which I had to mix into a gallon of water. I had to drink the whole thing five hours prior to the urine test. It was awful."

But it worked. After she passed the urine test, Tori was handed a plane ticket to Chicago. She was off to boot camp.

For the next two weeks, until her day of departure on April 19, 2000, Tori spent all her time getting high. Tori was relieved that while she had to tell her mother that she had lost her job, at least she could tell her she now had other plans. "My mother was already mad because I was actively using at that time and had stolen money from her to buy drugs and told me I had to leave the house," Tori says. "When she saw my plane ticket, she almost shit. 'What did you do, you stupid SOB!' she yelled. 'Do you have any idea what this means? But maybe they can fix you. I can't. I'm done. If you go on the plane, you can't come back.' As high as I was, I understood how she felt."

Tori spent the rest of her time in Southie using drugs to escape. When she told the recruiter there was no way she could pass the next urine test, he simply brought her another one of those mysterious drinks which had previously allowed her to pass. "I was high when I got on the plane," Tori says. "But in boot camp, you don't have the option to be dope sick. There are no sick days. Of course, I had physical withdrawals, but I had no choice but to get through each day as best I could."

It didn't take Tori long to make friends at Naval Station Great Lakes where she spent fourteen weeks at boot camp involved in conditioning, marching, drilling, hands-on training, basic seamanship, shipboard communication, and fire-fighting skills. "We worked out all the time," Tori says. "I thought detoxing would be much worse than it actually was. The constant physical exercise helped me through my withdrawals. Plus I think being in a completely different place for the first time in my life, away from the streets and its temptations, away even from my family, distracted me from the discomfort. We were kept in good shape, eating three meals a day, and kind of building up our strength. It wasn't like you could just quit boot camp. Once you were in, the only way out was a medical discharge. What was tough for me was running since I was never much of a runner. But once I was out of boot camp and an enlisted, I could choose the exercise I wanted, and for me it was swimming, which, like all the McGuires, I had done all my life."

With drugs no longer a part of Tori's life while she was in boot camp, she felt stronger physically than ever before. It didn't take long before she became comfortable with the other recruits there. Tori enjoyed the fact that the younger guys at boot camp gravitated toward her, finding her a motherly type. When she saw some of them crying or acting like young boys, she told them, "You need to get your shit together. Remember you're now property of the Navy and you will be a target so don't start crying."

She told them it was like a jail house mentality in the military and that if they started crying, everyone would have to run laps and would hate them. "I was coming from a place of realness and compassion, and they ended up listening to me," Tori says. After boot camp, Tori moved on to A School, not far from boot camp in Chicago, where she spent nine weeks before heading to C School in San Diego for nineteen weeks of training to become a medic. To Tori, it was almost like becoming a triage nurse or a paramedic where she would have to make an immediate assessment on an incoming patient. She learned to take blood, set up IVs, treat broken bones, and do CPR, all of which she found she enjoyed.

With no problem, Tori passed all the physical and written tests to meet the qualifications for rank, ultimately becoming a first class Petty Officer, stationed on an amphibious ship, USS Boxer (LHD 4), situated on 32nd Street in San Diego. At C school, she encountered older people like chiefs and ensigns and other enlisted officers, some of whom were her training officers. She understood that these officers were not supposed to interact with a lowly new recruit like her and was surprised that some of the older officers, as well as the ones close to her age, drifted toward her. "Maybe it was because, even though I wasn't actively taking drugs during that time, they could still see I was a fucking train wreck and that I didn't give a shit," Tori says. "Some guys were mean to newer recruits but not to me. I'd made it clear that I didn't want to play any games with anyone. And I didn't back down and wasn't afraid of anyone. That, if necessary, I could drop you where you stand, outrank or no outrank. That was my Southie mentality, and I guess it showed."

While Tori was avoiding any drugs during those weeks of training, she was surprised at how different the drug practices in the Navy were from what she was used to in Boston. "Here in C School some did drugs out in the open," Tori says. "Back at home, I wouldn't let anyone know what I was doing. Also here some people were charging too much. In the Navy, drinking was allowed and even encouraged. They wanted us to socialize with one another. They pushed for military marriages, which made it more likely the couple would remain in the military for longer periods of time."

From the beginning, Tori had no trouble identifying the people who used drugs. "To me, they stuck out like a sore thumb," Tori says. "For the first six months, I didn't drink or do drugs. After fourteen weeks in boot camp, I was still a bit of a mess, constantly aware that I was still experiencing some withdrawal problems, but I had also never felt as physically or mentally good. When I did start to drink, because everyone else did, I just drank a small amount. I knew I was going to put on weight anyhow since the food had so many carbs in them. Now I didn't care about the empty calories of alcohol. I just wanted the emotional relief. But now I also knew how it felt to be sober and I liked it. I saw that lots of the recruits smoked grass, but I knew grass was harder to mask when you had random drug tests. Plus, the high didn't last for me. After four or five drugs tests, I was pretty much squared away with these drug tests, which would only come infrequently when my particular number came up."

Having gone to religious schools until high school, Tori considered her religion and her relationship to God of immense importance in her life. Even in the toughest moments in her life, her deep belief in God stayed strong. In the Navy, she'd been picked to be the religious petty officer in the barracks. "They would all see me on my knees in the morning," Tori says. "And most of them would say, 'Hey, Donlan, we would never have guessed.'"

The Bad Ass Goes to Baghdad

In C School, after nine months in the Navy, after completing her training for medic, Tori was deployed to Baghdad on USS Boxer (LHD 4). There were 4,000 personnel on the ship, including 600 women, who slept in barracks with three tiers of coffin-like bunks in each barrack. "I told them I was too new to be deployed, but they said it was no problem, that they would figure it out," Tori says. "They told me I would learn by doing everything. I thought it was pretty cool to get deployed as a medic 45 miles off the coast of Kuwait on this amphibious carrier. I had nothing to lose, and I think that attitude showed up as courage or fearlessness instead."

On the ship, or in a tent off the ship, Tori was treating

soldiers who were often severely injured. "We either tagged them with triage when they were still living or bagged them into bags when they weren't," Tori explains. "Immediately, we would have to prioritize them according to their injuries. For some new medics from Tennessee, it was pretty traumatic to view these injuries. But I had seen a lot in my own neighborhood of South Boston, from suicides to people being beaten up or shot, so I didn't fall apart at what I was seeing."

As a medic, Tori administered morphine patches to the men who were heading off the ship to use as pain pills if needed. And it didn't take long until a lot of these morphine patches fell into her own hands. Tori could figure out the lot number and keep it in order, so it wouldn't show up until someone else was on the book. "I would shoot the morphine into my thigh and a warm rush would go through my body," Tori says. "I might have an itchy sensation, but instantly I would feel good and would be filled with energy. At first I was using it maybe a couple of times a month, but then it was a couple of times a week until finally even more often than that. I could figure out how to cook the books and fly under the radar with it. I figured I was smarter than everyone there. Once I figured out a system with the books, no one realized the gaps. I hit myself off with the morphine, like it was an EpiPen."

As a result of 9/11, everything had become more intense at Tori's station as the ship had been put under high alert. Tori worked harder as the injuries she treated continued to grow even more serious. "While we were not under heavy fire, convoys were being blown up," Tori says. "We still treated Marines for heat exhaustion, but I would see seventeen-year-olds without their legs, and we had to get them immediately onto a stretcher and into the helicopter."

Tori believed that using morphine helped her become a more capable medic. "It made me smarter," she says. "I was a more aware functioning addict. I did my job extremely well. My military jacket showed my advancement as I made rank and got accommodations very fast. I don't think you realized the pull this stuff has on you until the damage is done. With the morphine, I was able to bury some of the stuff I saw, and you don't even remember half the stuff or the trauma until later when it hits you at a very hard time."

West Coast Wasteland

After the nine months in Baghdad, USS Boxer (LHD 4) returned to its home port on 32nd Street in San Diego. "Usually you had eighteen months before you were deployed again, but this time we were to be in San Diego for only six weeks until we would be deployed, this time to Kuwait," Tori says. Things were different for Tori when her ship pulled into port. Once in a while she would leave the ship and shower in an apartment rather than on the ship. Anxious when she came ashore, Tori was more comfortable back on the ship where she was well respected. She felt like she no longer knew how to do anything if she wasn't on the ship.

Though Tori kept in touch with her family back in

Boston, she had no desire to go home for those six weeks. Just the thought of leaving San Diego to go home made her nervous. Even though she had always been deeply close to her family, she believed they were all better off with her far away from them. "I knew they were all so proud of me, but I still felt I was a shitcase, a fraud," Tori says. "I knew I had hurt them before I left. I had so much remorse for all I had done to them, how I had even robbed them before I left. Now they were praising me every time we talked, but I was so worried about how I would act if I went home and what a disappointment I would be to all to them. I knew I was a fraud in the military, no different than when I had been snorting heroin at home."

Whenever Tori did go off the ship with her friends, she ended up at a house party in San Diego frequented by some Mexican kids. "As a white woman, I was already a minority in the military, but I found that black and Mexican kids were attracted to me," Tori says. "At the party, some people were smoking crystal meth, and they kept asking me if I wanted some. I'd never used it before. My friend Samantha kept telling me I had already had my drug test so there would be no problem but I still decided not to try it."

The entire week after the party, Tori found herself thinking about meth a lot. When she returned to the house where the party had been, she asked the kids there about it. "I knew enough to ask them where they cut it," she says. "If you snort, it is more dangerous depending on where you cut it. If you cook it and smoke it, you can cook the stuff out of it. I told them to level with me, that

I needed to know if I could shoot it or snort it or smoke it. The kid I was talking to knew what was going on and respected me because I was a sharp shooter. The first time I had it there, I ended up smoking it in a pipe."

When her friend Samantha was killed in a car crash after she left that house one night, Tori was devastated. Losing her closest friend in the Navy was as mind numbing as the realization that had Tori left the party with her, she might also be dead. When Tori thought of everything she had seen while on the ship and now Samantha's untimely death, life seemed so fragile.

For the next few weeks while Tori was stationed in San Diego, she returned to the same house where she was able to connect with the same kid whom she trusted. "I got his number and he was cool and got the stuff for me," Tori says. "He wasn't military, and I didn't want to be ratted on by the military so it worked out fine for us. I had made a new friend who had the goods and because I had made rank and had more freedom, I had no problem connecting with him. The day I learned we were being deployed to Kuwait, I told him I would need a good amount to use for the four days on the ship to get there. He had no problem doing that for me."

Also, while Tori was in San Diego, she reconnected with guy from her boot camp who had decided to become a Navy Seal. "When we had ran into each other at boot camp, I would act out sexually with him," Tri says. "I can easily shut off being with people, telling them not to call me. I made it clear that I was not looking to snuggle with anyone or fall in love with them, that I was damaged enough to shut it off whenever I wanted to. I said that if you can't do it this way, let's break it off or you will be hurt. This guy did understand. He kind of liked me and said I was the coolest girl he had ever met. I felt I was better off sleeping with one guy than with twelve other guys."

On the way to Kuwait, the ship stopped in Hawaii and then in Australia for some liberty. When Tori arrived in Australia, she checked and found out the guy from her boot camp was there as well. "I was with him for two days, then said goodbye and took off," Tori says. "In Kuwait, I was smoking crystal meth all the time, still cooking the books and doing morphine."

One day, five months after she'd arrived in Kuwait, Tori fainted in the desert. "They took some blood from me back on the ship which sat 40 miles off the coast," Tori says. "After that, the military police came over to me and said my commanding officer wanted to talk to me. I was sick to my stomach. They had zero tolerance for drugs. I couldn't fucking believe this was happening."

But when Tori went to see her commanding officer, he told her hCG had come up in her urine, indicating she was pregnant. "I told him that was impossible, that I haven't done anything for five months." But the officer told her they were flying her to Germany for gestational growth to see exactly how far along she was. Tori knew that if she were more than three months pregnant, she would have no other option except to keep the baby. She also understood that no pregnant servicewoman could remain on board after the twentieth week of pregnancy while the ship was in port. Members discovered to be pregnant while deployed were to be transferred ashore as soon as possible under Navy rules. If she were more than four months pregnant, she knew they would send her back home.

In Germany, Tori learned that she was indeed five and a half months pregnant and no longer in the Navy. "I couldn't believe it," Tori said. "I was terrified. I had been doing drugs and had had no prenatal care. And there was no option to get rid of the baby." And so, 19 months after she had left South Boston, and five-and-a-half months pregnant, Tori was going home.

Tori knew that when she did get home, she would have to see a JAG (Judge Advocate General) lawyer and manage to get a medical discharge clearing the way for her to receive the military benefits that she had earned during those nineteen months in the Navy.

The Mother of All Miracles

But the discharge concern was far from Tori's greatest worry. As she kept reminding herself, she was more than five months pregnant, had no prenatal care, and was still on drugs. "I was terrified," Tori says. "I had always loved kids and had secretly prayed that someday I would be a mother. My sister Lanie always said that the reason I loved children so much was because I was childlike myself. And she meant it as a compliment. Now all I knew was that once again I had disappointed my family. Now I was pregnant and out of the Navy."

Heartbroken that she would have to relate yet another failure, Tori had called her mother and given her the bad news. Elaine Donlan had immediately sent her daughter a plane ticket, assuring her they would work things out. Grateful for her mother's support, Tori still worried about telling her maternal grandmother Elaine Sweeney McGuire whom she adored.

"I was so ashamed," Tori says. "When I went to see my Nana, she was so happy that I had come home. When I told her about my situation, that I had been knocked up and was expecting her first great grandchild, she said, 'What the hell are you crying about? You are beautiful. This is nothing to be ashamed of. Don't worry about a husband. You don't need a husband to raise a child. You are strong enough to do it yourself. Just get over it. I will always love you.'"

Tori considers her grandmother's reaction a pivotal moment both in their relationship and in her life. She had always been careful to hide the fact that she was on drugs from her grandmother. Yet, she was sure some part of her grandmother knew, and it had to have been very painful for her. "She hated it when my mother drank and would say, 'Put down that goddamn bottle,'" Tori says. "My mother covered for me around her. I couldn't have loved my Nana more. If she believed I could get through this horrible problem, then I would. I just knew then that God had our stories written. And this was mine."

Indeed, throughout all her problems with drugs, Tori clung to her religious beliefs. "My grandmother used to say this kid is a pain in the ass," Tori says, "but the one thing she has done right is God. I knew exactly what she meant and she was right."

Back at home, Tori's next step was to go to a South Boston health center, where she met a midwife. "I told her I was a junkie and had taken heroin and occasional meth," Tori says. "And had no prenatal care. She asked if I was high then, and, totally honest, I said no. She said from all the tests, it appeared as if this baby was okay. I told her I had left here a piece of shit, a raging, heroin addict. She asked if I was going to use now. I told her I didn't want to, but I was transitioning back to civilian life and it wasn't easy."

When the midwife told Tori she needed to be put on an anti-depressant, Tori refused, insisting she would abuse it. "But this woman wasn't judging me," Tori says. "She gave me her number. And I needed to be honest. I knew that Southie was a great place to get high, but now I saw it was an even better place to get sober."

Tori soon joined AA, and through a childhood friend she met there, she also met his roommate Dan Sullivan from Charlestown, ten years her senior. "Sully became my boyfriend and best friend for eleven years," Tori says. "We started dating while I was pregnant."

On December 16, 2004, Tori, twenty-seven, went into premature labor at thirty-one weeks. "I couldn't believe that my baby girl, delivered by C-section, was the picture of health," Tori says. "Considering my drug use in the Navy, the drinking to help me make rank faster, the morphine patches, the cocaine, and the crystal meth, as well as heroin, there was no way I could not have damaged my baby. Except by the grace of God, there was absolutely no reason my daughter should have been okay. My daughter was a gift from God. I will never not be grateful for her, and I give Jesus all the glory for her."

Once Tori got her discharge settled, she was able to receive separation pay to stay home with her baby for eighteen months. "I couldn't believe how lucky I was to have such a beautiful child as Mackenzie," she says. "I knew I had to give an honest effort to get clean, or else I would kill myself so my mother could raise her."

Tori also knew it would be dangerous for her to stay indefinitely at her mother's house where her mother would do everything for her. She needed to get strong and sober to take care of her daughter herself. "My mother was so welcoming and non-judgmental," Tori says. "She was the type that if you killed someone she would help you bury him. But when I got home, I was so beaten down. I didn't have any connection to dealers because I had screwed so many dealers in the past. I was just a wreck. I didn't know how to talk to people. I had no hustle left. I didn't want either to live or to get high any more."

Tori's contacts at the Gavin House for men sent her to the Edwina Martin House, a twenty-one-bed residential drug and alcohol treatment facility for women in Brockton. "When I got there, I told the first woman I met that I was a master manipulator and that I needed to do something to change," Tori says. "They took me in."

Tori and Mackenzie were supposed to be there for six months, but because Mackenzie walked early and the House was not insured for walking children, they had to leave. "I had just been getting sober for four months then," Tori says. "And I knew that if I went home, I would sabotage that."

Luckily, Tori found an opening at a homeless shelter in Cape Cod, the Angel House in Hyannis. The one stipulation to her moving there with Mackenzie was that DSS would now have to be involved in her life. "The director said I didn't have the correct background to get in there since I hadn't been abused, but they decided I was worth it and would give me a chance," Tori says. "My mother was so angry with me for going there rather than staying with her that I had to sneak out all of Mackenzie's things while she was at work. She loved me and the baby, and her intentions were good, but she was naive. I had to leave. I couldn't stay there and get the help I needed."

Tori and Mackenzie remained at the Angel House for thirteen months. By then, Mackenzie was two years old and Tori was clean. And she still is today.

From Southie to Sobriety

Tori's memories of her drug-filled years are never far from her memory. "I know that I had a charmed life and a loving wonderful childhood with the best parents imaginable and a tribe of cousins and incredible aunts and uncles and yet I still had a drug problem," she says. "I caused my family so much pain then and had a deep spiritual decay, but they kept loving me and saw my worth. But I am a different person now. I see the way the drug epidemic touches everyone in all economic and social levels. I had all the blessings of life but I couldn't get out of my own way."

Today, Tori maintains a strict vigilance in her own life and never hesitates to tell anyone that she is in recovery. "I was on drugs from ages nineteen to twenty-seven, for eight years, and now I have been sober longer than I was ever high," she says. "Back then using was a kind of life and the norm for me. It is not that way anymore. But I still have respect for how powerful drugs can be. I know I am one bad decision away from being right back there. It is not as if I ever think I would like to have the taste of a beer or I want some heroin to make me feel better. I recognize that would be an easy thing to do, but it is the last thing I would ever consider. It would be sure death for me. I feel as if my whole generation is being wiped out. When we hear about another death from heroin, we are becoming even more desensitized to it. And that is awful."

Tori recently dealt with the heartbreaking heroin death of a friend. Tori spent hours with her friend's family the day she died. "Her mother kept telling me I was beautiful and that Mackenzie is beautiful and how proud she was of me," Tori says. "But I honestly think I have survivor's guilt. Why should I be alive when so many others have died from what I once did?"

Tori remains eager to talk to those suffering from addiction whenever she has the opportunity. Her advice to those facing this crisis is to seek a spiritual solution and maintain constant vigilance, to reach out to other people. "Personally, I credit my recovery to a power greater than me," she says. "I'm a very spiritual person. My connection with God is the one relationship in my life that has always come easy, even as a little girl. God's grace is an unmerited gift that none of us deserve but all of us are surrounded in."

Tori's relationship with her now twelve-year-old daughter is, unquestionably, the most important and joyous aspect of her life. "No matter where I was during my recovery, Mack was with me," Tori says. "I have always said she has an old soul. She knows about my struggles and is the first one to tell anyone that her mother doesn't drink because she is allergic to alcohol. Just the way some people are allergic to peanuts. And that is exactly the way AA describes alcoholism in the Big Book. The biggest thing to understand is that it is an allergy and not one that you can ever grow out of it. Of course, I worry that since we are so close and it is inevitable that even though Mack has seen the damage that drugs and alcohol have done, she will still experiment when she grows up. But I hope we will always have the open communication we have today. Whenever a problem comes up, I never pretend to have all the solutions. But I assure her that I love her and we will figure it all out."

Right now, Tori's pride in her daughter is unbounded. "I never had the self-confidence that Mack has," Tori says. "Not only is she always on the honor roll, but she is an amazing athlete. I was a swimmer when I was younger. After all, to be a McGuire you have to be a swimmer. But I was overweight and never had her self-assuredness. She is on the AAU (Amateur Athletic Union) basketball team, plays soccer, softball, and is on a swim team. She even plays the viola and the guitar."

Tori is adamant that, as much as she loved growing up in Southie, she would never want to raise her daughter there now. "It's just not the same neighborhood now that it was back then," she says. Tori thinks that in many ways Southie got a bad rap, that it was always known for its loyalty and camaraderie, but people thought Southie women were rough around the edges. "We weren't," she insists. "We just got it. We conduct ourselves with a bit of a swagger. I consider it a badge of honor to be from Southie."

Of one thing concerning Southie, however, Tori is very clear. "In no way is Southie to blame for my drug use," she states firmly. "I made the choices. Bad things might have happened to me there. But it was a city and there were lots more people and lots more opportunities for things to go wrong. We saw so much more there. There were always police cars and fire engines but none of that stressed us kids out. We were used to it. It was a melting pot with much more diversity than in the suburbs. But living there, you saw stuff and you had to make decisions. I don't think it matters where you are. Drugs don't discriminate."

Tori knows that her cherished daughter may have to make decisions, and she can only hope she will make the right ones. "I hope she never has to deal with those demons, but she will never have to deal with them alone. I have so much faith in God so whatever her story turns out to be, I will be there."

Tori is also quick to admit that this past year has also been wrought with pain both for her and Mackenzie. For another vitally important part of Tori's recovery and present life has always been Dan "Sully" Sullivan. "He and Mackenzie have the most incredible bond that I have ever seen," she says. "I know that God not only placed him in her life but put her in his life so they could both experience true love."

However, sadly, after their wonderful eleven years together, Tori and Sully broke up in January 2016. "I guess our roads in life came to a cross road and we chose separate paths," Tori says. "While I am riddled with fear, I pray on it all the time and I know not to have 'stinking thinking.' I have responsibilities to Mack and all those who love me. I have no choice but to be okay, and I will be."

4. FAMILY IS EVERYTHING

THE ELAINE McGUIRE DONLAN STORY

"Hyannis had the Kennedys; Southie had the McGuires."
It's a bold statement, but when it comes to the vast
reach of this family's heritage, the McGuires have earned
their prominent position in Southie. Much has to do
with the size of this family. We met a fourth-generation
McGuire, Tori Donlan, previously, but understanding her
family history, and the journey taken by her own mother,
Elaine McGuire Donlan, offers a context beyond compare.
Through Elaine's vivid descriptions and recollections of a
childhood in Southie, we get a panoramic tour of the city
of South Boston, and a deeper look into the inner work-
ings of the customary way of life of a proud Irish family.

In fact, today, five generations of Southie men and
women stem from this family tree. Tori's mother, Elaine
McGuire Donlan, known to many family members as Baby
Elaine, is the oldest of ten children and is the namesake
of her mother, Elaine Sweeney McGuire. On the day she
died, at age eighty-five, Elaine Sweeney McGuire boasted
ten children, thirty-seven grandchildren and, at the time

of this writing, seven great grandchildren, including Tori's daughter Mackenzie.

Elaine McGuire Donlan, proclaims, "Once you have met one McGuire, you've met us all." Standing at a mere five foot one, stunningly pretty with dark hair and hazel eyes, Elaine Donlan is the picture of most of her striking McGuire relatives. But the McGuire reputation went far beyond just looking alike. And being exceptionally good looking. They were strong-willed activists, standing up vocally for justice and things they believe in—namely, what was good for the community of South Boston.

Grandma Fanny Sweeney was quite a woman in her own right. According to Elaine, her grandmother was influential in the political career of William Bulger, whose eighteen-year tenure as president of the Massachusetts Senate is the longest in history, and who was also president of the University of Massachusetts. "He went to her in the late fifties when he was first starting out and said he needed her help," Elaine says. "Fanny immediately set him up with her son Billy Sweeney and his best friend Will McDonough, a well-known sports writer for the *Boston Globe*. Together they ran his first campaign in 1960. And he won." Billy Bulger was also the younger brother of mobster James Whitey Bulger.

But Fanny's daughter Elaine Sweeney McGuire was no slouch when it came to speaking her mind and making a difference herself in the political world. When the school busing fracas ripped Southie apart in 1974 as court-ordered desegregation mandated that Southie students be sent to predominated black schools in Roxbury, while the black students in Roxbury traveled to South Boston, Elaine Sweeney McGuire joined ROAR (Restore Our Alienated Rights), an anti-desegregation busing organization formed by Boston School Committee Chairman Louise Day Hicks. Somehow, despite working a full-time job and raising ten children, Elaine Sweeney McGuire found the time to march in ROAR's protests, doing whatever she could to help the people in her city fight the unpopular plan.

During a trip to Ireland with her daughter Bernice and son-in-law Tom Irwin, Elaine Sweeney McGuire met three unkempt and dirty brothers asking for spare change. Though everyone else ignored the children, Elaine, talking lovingly to them, handed them her change and heralded them into an ice cream shop. Here, filled with anger for the shop owner's nasty behavior toward the children and her own unbridled empathy for the little boys, she bought them ice cream. "By this act, this singular act of civility, gentility, love and compassion, she illustrated the fundamental essence of our faith," Tom wrote in his loving eulogy for his mother-in-law. "Her ability to juggle so much probably stems from the fact that Elaine Sweeney was from a jumbo-sized family herself. Though two of her sisters died before she was born, Elaine Sweeney grew up as third generation Southie, with eight other siblings, including her twin brother Don, gleaning first hand experience when it came to raising extra-large families.

"As for my father's mother, Grandma McGuire, "I got

extra attention from her," Elaine says. "That was because I was the first and often the caregiver of my siblings."

Elaine Donlan and her nine brothers and sisters were raised on Grimes Street in Southie, two streets from St. Augustine's Parish and one street from St. Augustine's school, where many of the McGuire children attended school from grades one through twelve. The house on Grimes Street was four bedrooms, a living room, and a kitchen. "Four of us girls slept in one room," Elaine says. With ten children to care for, Elaine Sweeney McGuire kept the family ship sailing as smoothly as humanely possible, running the house with a strong hand. She had no choice. Her husband, Eddie "Red" McGuire, who died at age seventy-five in 2001, was a gentle lovable man, a Southie fireman, of Engine One. There was no way he was ever going to discipline his brood of ten. For Elaine, it was a happy childhood, though not without problems.

"My mother and I locked horns a lot and she beat the shit out of me the most," Elaine says. "There were many years when I made it my business to be out of the house when she was home and home when she was out."

Somehow, Elaine's mother even managed to work full time for the telephone company while she was raising ten kids. She would do the eleven-to-seven overnight shift, arriving home in time to get her kids out of bed, dressed, fed, and on their way to school.

"And, believe me, we were immaculate every time we left that house," Elaine says. "We were all dressed to the nines, looking like we walked out of the band box, us girls with long finger curls and bows in our hair, our school uniforms starched and spotless. It was part of the Southie mothers' mindset that their kids had to look perfect every time they left the house for school or for church. No matter how tired she was, our mother polished all our shoes and scrubbed our laces clean before she left for work at eleven every evening."

Red McGuire did all he could to be home for dinner every night, cooking that dinner himself many nights. "My father was a fabulous cook," Elaine says. "And so was my mother. All of us always had to be home for dinner, where every night someone spilled milk all over the place. I was always standing by the table with a towel in my hand."

No matter who was cooking, the McGuire family would have four-course delicious meals every night with no shortage of food. Insisting she would rather pay the butcher than the doctor, Elaine Sweeney McGuire never scrimped putting out healthy meals for her family. Since there would be more than enough food for extras, she encouraged her children to bring home friends, and there wasn't a friend who didn't clamor to get a seat at the crowded dinner table.

"There was a girl in my class who looked emaciated, so I made her a lunch every day," Elaine says. "I was the one who was making the lunches for all my siblings so it was no big deal to make one more. All our friends thought our house was a fun house and wanted to be there. The grass is always greener, so I wanted to be in their quieter houses."

Elaine insists there could not have been a better place in which to grow up than Southie. "It was a real community," she says. "Everyone knew everyone and everyone looked out for each other."

Even though she knew her mother didn't like it, Elaine "hung" in the Old Colony projects where all her friends lived. "As the oldest I had a reputation for taking care of my family and friends," Elaine says. "I made it especially clear that if you screw with my family, you're dead. I knew there were bullies around us but if anyone bothered my brothers and sisters, as the eldest of the family, I would have no problem rearranging them."

Elaine remembers well the day when she was 12 and got jumped by a bunch of neighborhood kids. She was returning home from getting some eggs and butter for her mother at the neighborhood grocery store. "All I kept thinking while these kids beat me up was that I had to protect the eggs. I knew how much they cost and hated to think of them breaking all over the street." When Elaine finally got home her face and clothes were covered with blood, but the eggs were intact. But her spirit was deeply shaken. Begging her father, who like so many men in Southie was an amateur boxer, to teach her how to fight, Elaine was determined this would never happen to her again. Thanks to him, Elaine learned the skills that made her, slight as she was, a powerful adversary to anyone who picked on her or any McGuire.

But it was Elaine's mother Elaine Sweeney McGuire, the matriarch of the family, who sent the most fear running through the veins of any kid in Southie, not just her brood of ten. "At any time of the day, my mother would come barreling into the projects in her blue beach wagon, yelling like hell looking for me, and everyone quaked, including me," Elaine says.

Stories abound in the family of the numerous times that their mother found taking care of ten kids even beyond her infinite energies. One morning, Elaine Sweeney McGuire wheeled the stroller to go to Bells, the neighborhood grocery store. When she came out of the store with her arms filled with groceries, she followed her usual routine of talking to every neighbor, or even stranger, she met, and simply walked home, forgetting all about the stroller. Her mind was most likely filled with thoughts of all she had to do before she left for work that evening. "I walked in that afternoon and found my mother half out the window, washing the windows with ammonia and water the way she did nearly every day," Elaine says. "All of a sudden, she yelled out, 'Jesus Christ, Elaine, that looks just like my carriage!' I looked out and sure enough, a neighbor Rita Graul, who was real influential in the church and the community, was pushing our stroller with Matty, who was six months old. I ran down and got him, carried him into the house and changed his diaper while he continued to sleep. All my mother could say was, 'Don't tell your father,' which I never did. But he found out anyhow. In our house you could never keep a secret. Truthfully, it might have been a bit weird to just leave a kid somewhere but it was perfectly safe to do that in Southie."

Another memorable McGuire moment occurred the

day Elaine's parents gathered all nine of their kids, (the final McGuire, Monica, was not born yet) into the Buick wagon for a ride to New Hampshire. When they all piled back into the car after leaving a gas station in Manchester, New Hampshire, their mother counted heads, and off they went with When they got to the Mystic River Bridges, one of the kids suddenly realized that Bernice, was missing. Their mother had counted nine heads in the back of the wagon, but one belonged to the neighborhood kid who had joined them. Red McGuire turned that car around and sped as fast as he could during the hour and a half ride back to the gas station, so distraught about his missing daughter that he nearly had a nervous breakdown. Not a single word was spoken that whole ride back to New Hampshire, but there was lots of sobbing as eight McGuire kids imagined life without Bernice.

"The man at the gas station sent us to the police station, where we found Bernice sitting on the counter, happily eating a bag of potato chips and a chocolate candy bar and sipping a Coke through a straw," Margie McGuire Shaughnessy says. "The minute we saw her we all stopped crying and started screaming at her to share her goodies. She would not."

Elaine admits that their mother handed out heavy physical discipline, that she was always ready to smack and hit and that there was never time with such a large family to sit down and discuss a problem. She solved them all by hitting. Some of her most famous lines were, "Come over here so I can break your neck," and "Remind me to beat you later." If she was on the phone and one of her kids did something wrong, she would simply throw the phone at the misbehaving child. When one of their children brought home a bad report card and tried to hide under her bed, she turned into Hercules, lifting up the bed so she could pull out the offending daughter and slap her. "She never ran out of reasons to hit us," Elaine says.

"As a result I have handled my family differently," explains Elaine. "I swore, unlike my mother, that I would never put my hands on my children the way she did. Sure, there were times during my three girls' teenage years when I had to leave the room or I would have killed them. Just the way I would kill anyone who hurt them. But I did not follow my mother's example."

Baby Elaine derives great joy in the fact that her three daughters, Lanie, Tori, and Alexandra, unlike her, were all blessed with the same beautiful red hair as their grandfather, although chances are they received that hair color from their own father, Franny.

"My father was the love of my life," Elaine says. "I loved my husband Franny dearly, but my father was my first and dearest love. He was, as people still say today, the best fireman to come out of Southie. They said he was the first man in and the last man out. The other firemen told each other, 'If you want to be safe, follow Red.' And he always had a second job, washing windows, doing whatever he could to bring in extra money. He was just the sweetest, nicest guy in the world. Never the disciplinarian my mother was."

The Catholic Paradox

Tori Donlan's devout faith is splashed throughout her own story, as she openly praises God for His guidance during any difficult times in her life and as a religious petty officer in the Navy. No doubt this faith was enriched by the parish and school she had attended for so many years, the same all of the Sweeney's before her attended. But Tori's mother wasn't as keen on the idea of spending her entire school life so close to home at St. Augustine's Catholic elementary and high schools. All Elaine Donlan wanted to do was to go to Southie High, but her mother was dead set against it. "She was sure I would get into trouble there, and she was probably right," Elaine says. "So she sent me to St. Augustine's. I would get thrown out every week but the pastor would bring me back and tell me, no matter what I did, I wasn't going anywhere else. And I never did."

The church itself occupied its own place in Massachusetts history. Built in 1818-1819, it was the oldest Roman Catholic church building in Massachusetts. Its cemetery, established in 1818, is also the state's oldest Catholic cemetery. The Gothic Revival Chapel was originally built as a crypt for the remains of Father François Matignon, the first Catholic priest to come to Boston from France. Everything changed, however, in 2002 when a clergy sex scandal broke out, in which 271 clergy, including permanent and visiting priests, pastors, chaplains, deacons, religious order clerics, and nuns, were accused of child sex abuse in the Boston archdiocese. The Archdiocese of Boston was forced to close the church because of mounting financial pressures, partly as a consequence of this scandal, during which criminal charges were brought against five Roman Catholic priests in the Boston area.

Elaine remembers her mother's anger and sadness when their church closed its doors in 2004. Her mother attended meetings, signed petitions, and did whatever she could to change the minds of those in charge, just like Grandma Fanny would have. While Elaine Sweeney McGuire would not discuss the clergy abuse scandal with her children, Elaine Donlan is outspoken about the attempt to sweep the scandal under the rug. "It was bull-shit to pretend it never happened."

Elaine was all too aware of how this catastrophe affected her classmates. "One boy who was a good friend of mine when we were twelve told me what happened to him," Elaine says. "I'd known him since we were in the first grade and even though he could be a real pain in the ass, he began acting out real bad. When I kept asking him what was wrong, he finally told me that our fifth-grade teacher, a nun who was a real son-of-a-bitch and we all hated, had sexually abused him. I couldn't believe what I was hearing, but I knew he was telling the truth. I was so sick that I couldn't even move. I didn't say anything to anybody about it but a few days later, I just couldn't control myself. It was my nature and reputation to defend people, especially when they had been wronged, so I was sitting there still seething when I gave the nun some smart ass answer that I knew who would set her off."

But the nun's response shocked even Elaine. In an

instant, the nun had pulled her out of her seat, grabbing her by the hair and punching her face, bloodying her nose and mouth. When Elaine tried to get away from the blows, the nun grabbed her blouse, ripping off a section. Blinded by blood and rage, Elaine raced home, certain her mother would be at work. To her surprise her mother was not only home that day, but was filled with compassion for her daughter. Whenever there had been a former incident with a nun, Elaine Sweeney McGuire was old school, insisting that the nun was always right and one of her ten children was always wrong. This time, however, her anger was directed wholly at the nun. "She called me honey for the first time ever," Elaine recalls, "and led me back to the school. 'Look what you did to her!' she screamed at the nun, who looked good and frightened. My mother could beat me up, but no nun would ever be allowed to bloody my face and rip my clothes. That was the first and only time my mother ever came to that school, and the first and only time she ever went to bat for me."

After the visit, the principal immediately transferred Elaine into a different fifth-grade classroom, led by Sister Mary Catherine. Certain this nun would hate her for what she had done to her former teacher, Elaine was surprised when her new teacher pulled her aside and told her she was proud of Elaine for standing up for her friend. "I told her I wasn't afraid of that mean nun or any other nun and that I really wanted out of the school. But she put me at ease and said she would always be there to talk to me, and she was. She is the nun that got me through to graduation."

The following school year, the nun who had abused Elaine's friend did not return. "I believe Father O'Connor, the pastor of St. Augustine's, got rid of her," Elaine says. "Some of those nuns were vicious, frustrated women, and they took out their rage on innocent children. There were a few wonderful nuns that my friends and I loved, like Sister Mary Catherine, but too many of them were hateful. The saddest part of the story about my friend is that nine years later, when he was twenty-one, he killed himself."

Today, St. Augustine's church has been converted into a new condominium building featuring twenty-nine one, two, and three bedroom luxury condos, which range in price from $649,000 to $1.29 million. Advertisements for the Residents of St. Augustine offer the following advantages: "Located steps from Andrew Square and the Red Line Andrew T Station, the Residences at St. Augustine is close to numerous area amenities and shopping. The area amenities include, Stats Bar & Grille, Lincoln Tavern & Restaurant, several Banks and Boston's largest outdoor shopping mall, the South Bay Mall. South Bay includes stores and restaurants such as Target, Stop & Shop Supermarket, Best Buy, Home Depot, Panera Bread, Olive Garden, Bank of America and more. Everything you need is within walking distance, which makes this one of the most convenient neighborhoods in the city of Boston."

For Elaine Donlan, hindsight has made her more nostalgic for the school and parish she claimed to disdain as a child, creating quite the paradox. "I cry whenever I drive by that area," she says. "My babies were baptized there, I made my baptism and confirmation there, my sisters and I were married there. Every important aspect of our life took place at St. Augustine's."

When the steeple of the church was removed in 1985, Elaine felt a profound sorrow. The steeple's bell had so faithfully marked time for her during her childhood. "All my brothers and sisters would know when it was time to go home when that bell rang out the hours," she says. "If it was ringing five bells, we would race home for dinner. If it rang out nine, we sure as hell better get home fast."

Another building, which proved a vitally important part of all the McGuire kids' lives, was the South Boston Boys & Girls Club around the corner from Grimes Street. A second home to all ten of the children and a lifesaver for their mother, it was here they played games, learned sports, and made life-long friends. Although it was their mother who taught them to swim at the Lagoon at Pleasure Bay beach in Southie, it was at this club's pool where they spent so many hours perfecting their strokes and becoming excellent swimmers.

"I was on the club's swim team at age six and won just about every meet I was ever in. I even swam on the AAU swim team when I was eight for a few years," Elaine says. "But that was just a part of it. All us kids spent so much time down there. Every Friday night we would all head down there, bringing the required canned goods for the needy, and hang out and have a ball."

A major part of the Friday night event was a splash party which included a race for the girls and another one for the boys. Since Elaine always won the girls' race and

Norman Richards always won the boys' race, they decided to have a race between the two of them. Sometimes Norman won; sometimes Elaine did. But, no matter who won, there was always a lot of cheering and a lot of fun.

"We spent our summers there, out of trouble and having a great time," Elaine says. "They had the most phenomenal staff there. When I was there, the boys and girls clubs were separate. Today they are joined. It was so typical of our childhood in Southie, full of a caring, friendly, hardworking staff where kids could feel welcome any time we walked through its doors. In many ways, it created our feelings of comfort and happiness growing up in Southie and made all of us kids into the people we are today. And the club even saved the lives of some kids from the projects who didn't have enough food at their own homes and were fed with little fanfare at the club."

A New Generation of Her Own

Elaine had met the second great love of her life, Francis Xavier Donlan, known to all as Franny, when she was seventeen. It was not love at first sight, on her part anyhow. "Actually, Franny was born in Southie, but his father sent him to schools outside of Southie in order to keep him out of trouble," Elaine says. "I guess not everyone thought it was the top prize in the world to capture a Southie girl, though I can't imagine why. Franny's parents even moved to Canton when he was eleven and sent him to camp every summer. And what does he do? He marries a girl from Southie."

Not that Elaine McGuire made it easy for Franny Donlan, but, luckily, Franny was not the type to give up easily. He pursued Elaine for a month. Working up on a pole for the telephone company, Franny even managed to intervene in Elaine's phone calls. There was no escaping him. In 1970, three years after their first date, they were married at St. Augustine Church almost one year after Elaine Sweeney McGuire, at the age of forty, gave birth to her last child, Monica.

The wedding of the McGuire's first child was a highly celebrated Southie event with 375 people invited to a sit-down dinner and open bar at Florian Hall. "My parents hardly drank," Elaine says. "I never saw them drink in our house but that day and night there was even tons of food in our house, along with alcohol. We'd never seen that much liquor in our home before."

For the first eighteen years of their marriage, the Don-lans lived in South Boston, the only place the two of them ever considered as a home for their own family. Even though Elaine was out of school and married during the era of busing, some of her younger brothers and sisters were affected by the difficult situation. "St. Augustine had closed its school in nineteen-seventy-one, so all my siblings were mostly in public schools then," Elaine says. "One of my sisters ended up living in Belmont with another sister so she could go to school there. Louise Day Hicks was a true hero then, and so was Mayor Flynn. If I'd had a gun, I would have killed that Judge Garrity. He did terrible damage to our city by coming down with that ruling. He gave Southie an unfair reputation as a racist place where everyone hated blacks. And that just was not true. We all got along."

Even though she was not personally affected by the busing situation at the schools, one day Elaine found herself in a serious busing-related situation. Walking with her first-born daughter, Lanie, asleep in a beautiful pram, Elaine was returning from an afternoon at Carson Beach with some friends when she ran into a bunch of teenage boys at the bottom of Grimes Street. The boys, most of whom were friends of her brothers and sisters, were suddenly approached by a couple of policemen who looked anything but friendly.

"The streets were filled with policemen who were not local cops, supposedly to keep the peace during the confusion of busing, but seemed to be making things far worse. So I went up to the kids and told them to get the hell out of there, that these bastards would kill them for no reason," Elaine says. "Those cops were huge and had their clubs out. I knew they weren't our local police. I figured they were from the Tactical Police Force that was all over Southie supposedly to keep the calm, but doing nothing but making more trouble for all the people in our town."

Suddenly, the policemen were yelling at Elaine, telling her to get the hell out of there or keep her mouth closed or they would take her "fucking carriage." Never one to keep her mouth closed, Elaine went right into their faces, telling them in her own spicy language that if one of them put so much as a finger on that carriage their names and pictures would be all over the front page of every paper. Luckily, a local cop who knew her came racing over and got her away from the scene. "Three of those poor kids ended up getting beaten up and then arrested for doing nothing besides just standing there," Elaine says.

To Elaine, that incident typified her inherited righteous indignation toward all that was happening in Southie during that period. "It was all just so insane," she says. "The way those cops treated those kids that day and all the kids throughout South Boston made me sick to my stomach. It also just made me love Southie even more. We were the only ones who had the guts and courage to stand up for our kids and for our community. Others living in Dorchester or Roxbury didn't do as much as we did. But in Southie, all the families were saying, 'Leave our kids alone.' There was a huge anti-busing march with about five thousand mothers and fathers delivering the same message. And there was that unfortunate and misrepresented picture of Joe Rakes standing over the black man on the ground in another anti-busing march. The photo didn't show what was really happening that day. But it was typical for the press to do whatever it could to make Southie look like a crazy racist town. But in the long run it just made our camaraderie stronger. We knew the truth: that we were so much better than that."

Leaving Southie

In 1988 as a result of a poor investment, Elaine and Franny were forced to sell their house, as well as several other properties they owned in Southie and move to a Donlan family property in Canton. "It was a tough time for us, losing all that property," Elaine says. "Leaving Southie just about killed me. We ended up living in Canton for nine years, and, like me, my two oldest girls, Lanie and Tori, hated it there. They always considered themselves Southie girls and took the train back to Southie to stay with their aunts and uncles every chance they could. Believe me, I hated doing that to them, and to myself as well, but we had no choice financially."

Sadly, Franny became ill two years after they moved to Canton. "I have always been a caregiver," Elaine says, "so I had no problem caring for him at home even after he grew sicker and unable to care for himself."

Elaine's marriage to Francis Xavier Donlan, a plumber, a fireman and an arson inspector for the fire department, was a loving one that ended far too soon. "We were married for twenty-five years, two months and twelve days when he passed in nineteen-ninety-five, surrounded by all the McGuires and my girls and me," Elaine says. "My family shocked us with a surprise twenty-fourth anniversary party with over 200 people. They never thought Franny would last long enough for our twenty-fifth. I'll never stop loving that man."

Two years after Franny's death, Elaine and the girls were able to move back to Southie to the big house on Broadway. However, five years later, in 2012, Elaine, unable to continue to pay the expenses of the big house, moved to Braintree, a Boston suburb eleven miles from Southie. Here she would be nearer to her mother who was then living with her youngest sister, Monica, as well as to her daughter Tori and granddaughter Mackenzie.

Elaine is far from happy with all the changes that have taken place in Southie over the past twenty plus years, one of which included the loss of her parish church. "I was so fortunate to grow up in that wonderful town," she says. "We had the nicest people you'd ever want to meet. I never saw other communities get together to raise money when someone in the town needed it. But I think everything changed when the Tall Ships (an international regatta of gigantic multi-sailed ships) first came to Castle Island in South Boston in the late nineteen-seventies. Before then people wouldn't come near the place. But now everyone had a chance to see what a gem South Boston was, and rents became astronomical and you couldn't get a goddamned parking space in the town. The apartment I lived in during the eighties, with its two floors, is now going for five thousand a month."

However, despite the real estate changes, Elaine, now sixty-seven, expects to move back to Southie in the near future. She remains close with eight friends who were classmates at St. Augustine's fifty years ago and who still live in Southie. The nine women make a point of going away for weekends many times a year, as well as spending many fun days together in Southie Even though she complains bitterly about the impossibility of finding a decent parking space and the excessively high rents in Southie, she returns often, even to have her hair done.

"I will always consider myself a Southie woman," she says. "That is the only place where I want to live. My sister Margie still lives in Southie as does my sister-in-law. I love its beaches, my friends, all the pleasures I had growing up there and initially raising my girls there. How could I not want to live there? There's no place quite like Southie in the whole world. And somehow I always manage to get a parking space to go to Sully's or to Castle Island. It just takes some figuring out. I'm not exactly sure how I will do it but I will move back there in the not-too-distant future."

The Widowed Life

After Franny died, Elaine went to work for the prestigious Boston law firm of Finneran Byrne & Drechsler. For five years, she answered phones there, loving her job and the people with whom she worked. But problems with her knee necessitated a knee replacement, which turned out to be complicated by a contaminated knee. After five related surgeries to correct the problem, Elaine, unable to swim daily at the Boston Athletic Club, as she had always done, following in her mother's footsteps as a swimmer, found herself depressed and lonely, missing her husband more each day.

"We were all in pain after Franny died, and we all dealt with it in certain ways," Elaine says. "I found myself abusing alcohol at certain times. I was so sad that my middle daughter was tied up with substance abuse. I found myself unable to cope. I went to AA and started dating. I met one particular man who was clerk of the Senate for Billy Bulger. He was helping me a little bit with my daughter but I soon realized he had his own problems. One night I told him I needed to take care of my kids and myself and couldn't see him again. I wasn't in love with him the way I had been with Franny. When I went to leave the room...Boom. He blew his head off right in front of me."

Diagnosed with PTSD, both from the horrific violent death she had witnessed and from the long, difficult death of her husband, Elaine sought help. Her doctor put her on Xanax and suggested counseling, which she did for a while. Today, Elaine feels stronger, and although she will still have an occasional drink, she works hard to keep any alcohol problems in control.

"I have the hardest time living alone and not having anyone to take care of," Elaine says. "That was what I did from the day I was born. I was always a caregiver."

Elaine admits there are many hard moments when she remembers Franny. "I don't think I ever really grieved his death. Sometimes I weigh the odds of being lonely versus being in a relationship, and I'm not sure which is harder. But for now, I am lucky to have my three daughters and my beautiful granddaughter nearby. And, of course, all my brothers and sisters."

Even three years after her mother's death on July 10, 2015, Elaine is having trouble believing that this irrepressible and feisty woman is no longer here. For the first eighteen years of her marriage, while she was living in Southie and raising her daughters, Elaine spent many special hours with her mother and felt she got to know and love her differently than she had as a child living in her mother's tightly run house. Elaine treasured the advice and help her mother offered when she was learning how to care for three daughters and cherished their walks and shopping trips together.

"We're all still numb," Elaine says. "But we're all relieved she is not suffering and is with my dad again. They are both our angels now."

Elaine and her siblings lost track of how many people attended their mother's funeral service. "They had to close the highway for the huge crowd coming to the funeral and burial," Elaine says. "When my family was struggling to decide what to put on our mother's stone, some of my siblings wanted to put 'Duckie' on the stone, a nickname given to her by her twin brother Donald. She hated it with a passion! My Franny was the only one who could get away with teasing her with that name. But he could do no wrong with her. Finally, we all decided the headstone should read the words she told us often and up to the very end: *Always be good to one another.*

We all promised we'd try."

5. THERE GOES THE TEACHER LADY

THE MARIE FALCIONE HARDY STORY

When the Italian father of a dear friend was dying at New England Medical Center in downtown Boston, Marie knew he would hate the hospital food. "So I cooked him a little food and brought it to him," Marie said. "A little food" meant two shopping bags that she carried into the hospital room, one in each hand, as she announced, "I have brought lunch," to the delighted patient. As she unpacked the shopping bags, which she had carried on the bus and then lugged three long blocks to the hospital room, tears ran down the man's cheeks. But it wasn't just food that Marie carried in those two large shopping bags. There were also beautiful china plates, carefully wrapped, and shiny silverware, plus a long-stem wine glass. Lastly, Marie pulled out a small cassette player, pressed play, and sounds of Frank Sinatra singing "Fly Me To the Moon" filled the hospital room. Then she served delicious Italian foods—eggplant, homemade macaroni, and salad—as well as a large round Italian bread loaded with Italian cold cuts. "I knew this man never ate off of paper plates," Marie said, "and that meal time was sacred in his home, just like in mine."

With an Irish mother, Margaret, an Italian and father, Ernest, Marie Falcione grew up in the South End, along with her older sister Jean and her brother, Butchy, who was just eleven months younger.

In 1965, at age twenty, Marie married Jim Hardy, a South Boston fire fighter, as well as the head diver for the Boston Fire Department. Jim's father had died years earlier, but when Jim and Marie married, his mother, who was ill, and his three siblings, ages eleven, thirteen, and fifteen, moved in with the newlyweds. Jim's mother died shortly after the marriage but his sister and two brothers remained with them until each of them graduated from high school. Within a year of their marriage, Marie and Jim's first child, Jimmy, was born, followed by another son Tommy and their daughter Marie. The marriage was not a particularly happy one. Jim and Marie separated, and during a brief reconciliation attempt their daughter Melissa was conceived. Their divorce followed shortly.

While Marie might have complained about Jim's shortcomings as a husband, she raved about his competency as a firefighter. She was deeply proud of the way he had saved a three-year-old from a tragic fire. Because Jim had actually grown up in that same house, he managed to discover the little boy, badly burned on his face, lying in a tight ball in a staircase. Another fire fighter had thought the little body was a stack of newspapers. However, when Jim carefully and fearlessly rechecked each nook of the house, he managed to save the child's life, while putting his own in jeopardy, as the fire roared round him. "He might not have been the best husband in the world but he was the best fireman anyone could ask for," Marie often said. "You could never deny that."

Yet, even though Marie had a family of her own, when her mother, Maggie, became ill, she moved Maggie to her house to take care of her. Marie found much pleasure in having her mother live with her "On Friday nights, she would love going down to the local bar near our house," Marie said. "They played all these songs she liked and she would sing along right with them. She'd have maybe one or two drinks but Buddy, Marie's longtime partner, would have to piggy back her home afterwards. We had a lot of fun with her."

While Marie worked hard to care for her children and her mother, all four of her children fell prey to addiction. Marie's own addiction was cigarettes, a habit she used to cope with the stresses of motherhood and which she likely picked up from Maggie who died of COPD in 1986.

Still, despite her own stress and later health problems, Marie had established a reputation as the go-to woman for anyone who needed some extra help, or some extra cash. "There was always a family who didn't have a turkey for Thanksgiving or a Christmas tree for the holidays," Marie said. "I was more than happy to buy and deliver the turkey and all the fixings, or make sure a tree was delivered to the front door. It probably brought me more pleasure than it did to anyone else. You had to see the smiles I received. What a feeling."

When a close friend needed bail money for her son, Marie spent her lunch break at the local bank. An hour later, she handed her friend an envelope with ten crisp one hundred dollar bills. This was a large sacrifice for Marie, but her desire to help her friend left her no choice.

Working for Head Start for many years as an assistant teacher, Marie had no trouble finding out what student's mother needed help, then surreptitiously slipping a ten dollar bill from her own meager salary into the woman's coat as she left the school with her child. "When I was running the snack bar at the hockey rink, I got to know which kids couldn't afford the cocoa or a hot dog," she said. "It was no big deal to make sure those kids got whatever food they wanted. And maybe a little money in their pockets."

One of her co-workers at Head Start remembers vividly how Marie would sit the little ones on her lap and hand-feed them. If some of the kids were having separation anxiety, she would buy them children's watches and teach them how to tell time and figure out when Mommy would be coming to get them. "You had to see their little faces when they would look at those watches and try to figure out where the big hand should be when Mommy was coming," Marie said. "Everyone of them so precious."

Like many other Southie women, despite her own heartache, Marie had her hand on someone else's shoulder, comforting that person through personal agony. "I found that no matter how much someone was hurting, it made them feel good to hear a good joke and laugh,"

Marie said. "I just loved to see others practically collapse with rib-splitting laughter

Yet there was much in Marie's life that caused her endless tears. While all four of her children's additions brought their mother some pain, Melissa, her youngest, an exquisitely beautiful young woman with her own severe addiction problems, delivered the greatest heartache. "When Melissa became pregnant as a teen, I was devastated," Marie said. "But I listened to my own aunt who kept telling me, 'You're simply going to love this baby, feed it, bathe it and raise it.' And that's just what I did, thankfully with support from Buddy." Indeed, with her adored companion for thirty-five years, longshoreman Buddy Norton, by her side, Marie lovingly raised Melissa's son, Mackennan, known as Mac. "We really wanted to get married," Buddy says. "But my ex-wife was a Catholic and she wouldn't let us. I told her, 'You haven't been to church in 30 years,' but that didn't make a difference. But Marie and I were always together for all those years. We went everywhere together."

Neighbors often saw Buddy or Marie walking the baby around Castle Island well before six in the morning, gently placing his little feet in the ocean, wheeling him home to bathe him and feed him, keeping him loved and immaculate every hour of every day.

"While Buddy and I were raising Mac, Melissa was struggling, fighting her own demons in and out of rehab and in and out of jail," Marie said. "I never had any faith in Alcoholics Anonymous, which had never worked with any other members of my family."

For many years, Marie was fighting her own COPD with the same determination, as well as constantly cracking jokes, showing the good humor with which she had fought every one of her life's battles. Through all her treatments for her chronic lung disease and with her continuous need for oxygen, Marie still managed to maintain her own stunning looks. Her jet black hair was always cut in a modern updated style short, with fish hooks on the side, accentuating her delicate features, a small nose with huge greenish blue eyes, and full lips. She was never without her stylish white pearls or jade jewelry, contrasting with her striking olive skin.

All summer long, that skin would turn a rich golden brown, thanks to her daily walks around Castle Island, as well as the time spent at her home in Laconia, New Hampshire. "Jim and I bought this house up there many years ago," Marie said. "Even when the kids were little, we would spend the summers up there. I love everything there is about Southie, but New Hampshire is special in a different way. I've made lifelong friends up there. Whenever I'm feeling sick, I just have to imagine that cottage and before I know it, I'm out of the bed and in the car and headed up to the glorious New Hampshire air. I've never missed one summer at that special cottage, and I have no intention of letting that happen."

Tears of a Clown

After a loving Sunday visit with her mother at the Southie recuperation center on 6th Street where Marie was spending a few weeks to gain back weight and strength, her daughter Melissa placed a shiny Tory Burch bracelet on her mother's thin wrist. "She kissed me, told me she loved me, and, most important, she promised me she would not go back to the rooming house where she had lived with her estranged addict boyfriend to retrieve her belongings," Marie remembered. "That was the last time I saw my daughter alive."

Melissa had promised to call Buddy the next morning. When she didn't call on Monday, Buddy went down to the rooming house at East 4th Street see if she was okay. Finding the room padlocked from the outside, Buddy practically came to blows with the manager of the rooming house, who insisted he had seen Melissa and her boyfriend, Marty Jiminez, leave the apartment with packed bags on Sunday night. When Buddy reported what he knew was a lie back to Marie, she was equally furious, certain that Melissa no longer wanted to be anywhere near Marty and would never have just taken off with him like that. As it turned out, Jiminez, who had been driving Melissa's father's car, had been arrested on a DUI charge on Monday.

For the next two days, Buddy, accompanied by Melissa's brother and sister, pleaded with local police to break through the padlock or let him use his own bolt cutters to remove the lock. It was only after he reached a sergeant he knew from his years as a hockey coach that four Boston policemen, including a captain, arrived and finally broke the padlock blocking entry into the apartment. "Two minutes after the captain raced into the apartment, he came out and told me I couldn't come in, that I wouldn't be able to handle what I saw, that I would want to kill the person who had done this to Melissa," Buddy says.

Indeed, Melissa had been dead for three or four days by the time Buddy found her. She had been beaten to death with a baseball bat and hammer and her skull had been crushed. The only way she could be identified was by her dental records. Marty Jiminez pled guilty to second-degree murder and was sentenced to life in prison, but would be eligible for parole in fifteen years.

Somehow, Marie, gravely ill at the time, with the support of her sister Jean and Buddy, found the strength to select the Banana Republic silk dress in which her "baby" would be buried. "I remember so well the first Holy Communion dress I had ordered from Italy for Melissa on her special day so many years ago," Marie said. "Then I'd been able to protect my precious daughter from harm. She'd looked like a Southern belle that day. She had a wide-brimmed white hat, with her gorgeous blond banana curls spilling out from under the brim."

For Melissa's funeral mass at St. Brigid, the church where she had been baptized and made her first Holy Communion, as well as at her wake at O'Brien's Funeral Home and her burial at Cedar Grove cemetery in Dorchester, mourners from all walks of life gathered to pay their respects to a young woman whose life had been cut short by a brutal murder. "No one in Southie turns his back on an innocent victim like Melissa," Marie said. "Instead they all stand up for her and show their solidarity for one of their own. This horrible nightmare happened in Southie. She was one of ours. That's just the way it is here."

Southie Congressman Stephen Lynch, along with then Mayor Thomas Menino's right-hand man, Michael Kinneavy, were just a few of the dignitaries who stood beside ordinary Southie men and women saddened by the horrendous fate of a Southie young woman about whom they cared, even if they had never met her. It was such a horrific murder that everyone who heard of it felt some of the pain. It's a testament to the community of Southie not turning their backs on someone who had an addiction problem. They had all heard about her addiction problem, but that did not mean they cared any less about her. The way her neighbors saw it, Melissa was a young, beautiful mother who was human and had been struggling for so many years to overcome her addiction. That was more than enough for the people of Southie to mourn her tragic death. The fact that the Hardy's were well known in town because of Melissa's father's position in the fire department and Marie's role at Head Start were yet two more factors in the town's reaction to their daughter's death.

The pain that day was palpable, yet for Marie, sitting there absorbing each agonizing moment, tiny and frail yet composed, relying on her oxygen for every breath, the pain was not enough to make her close her eyes for good. "Someday I will be with her," Marie said. "But today Mac and Buddy still need me."

Outspoken even in her deepest pain, Marie did not hesitate to express her opinion that things might have been different if Whitey Bulger were still in Southie. "Crime escalated since he left," Marie said. "Marty Jiminez would of thought twice about killing Melissa then because he would of been dead before he was arrested."

After Melissa's death, most of Marie's family and friends were certain she would become sicker and would never leave the rehab. However, Marie surprised everyone, except for Buddy who never doubted her inner strength, by improving. She gained some weight and began to feel stronger, looking more like her old self, her makeup impeccable, her hair fashionably styled, every item of her wardrobe stylish. Family and friends often commented on her beauty and the fact that all men's eyes were still on her when she walked into a room, a fact lost on Marie.

Besides, she had other things on her mind, like her son Tommy, who had been by his mother's side numerous times when she was in the hospital. Tommy was the apple of Marie's eye, the "most loyal, hard working, sweetest, easiest child you could ever imagine," she repeated often. "That was before the drugs took over."

Tommy had two children, Kristen and Thomas. He'd been a successful carpenter, married to a lovely woman, and had once owned his own home, before he fell into the dark and fatal world of heroin.

A year earlier when Marie had been ill in her hospital room, she had woken to find Tommy sleeping on blankets on the floor next to her bed. "When I woke him and asked, 'What are you doing here?' he said he couldn't imagine his life without me in it," Marie said. "But he also told me he couldn't imagine me on life support, that he knew I'd never want to live with no quality of life. I'd told him he was right, that I would not want to be kept alive that way. He cried but he said he understood because he would never want that to happen to him either."

Marie was in rehab herself the night she had to make the decision to take her son off of life support when it was obvious he would never recover from a heroin overdose. Tommy had just returned from a short stint in prison earlier that day. He'd headed straight to Marie's house where Buddy had cooked him a large and delicious breakfast. He left Marie and Buddy to go to a welcome home party organized by his friends that evening. By ten that night he was dead. "As I sat in my room, all I could think of was the night he was so scared for me, for us both, to live without one another or see each other suffer," Marie said. "Never did I imagine that it would be me making the decision to take him off of life support. Never."

Giving Up Is for Sissies

After Marie lost Tommy, she showed yet again that giving up didn't exist in her vocabulary. Not when she lost her daughter nor her son. Not when Mac and Buddy needed her. It was that pride in Mac that pushed her onward every new day. She was so proud that before he went off to Bridgewater State, Mac spent the summer in Southie as a lifeguard. And that after Bridgewater, he transferred to Santa Barbara City Community College in California.

"When I look back to the day Melissa told me she was pregnant, I know now that that day proved the beginning of a blessing," she said. "I was fifty-two when I began to raise Mac, and I have loved every day I have been with him since. Mac is such a handsome and respectful young man, so much to be proud of. But I have to say that so much of the person Mac is today is due to Buddy who loves him every bit as much as I do and will always be his devoted father."

Marie was especially proud that Mac had been such a fine athlete, insisting that was because Buddy spent so much time with him. Buddy lights up when he discusses Mac. "He was good at ice skating and Pop Warner football and Little League," he says. "And he was a terrific boxer. Every year before on St. Patrick's Day they had boxing the Friday night before the parade. Mackie would flatten his opponent. He started when he was ten and he was a champion every year. By the time he was eleven, they couldn't find anyone in his age group to fight. He would have to fight fourteen-or fifteen-year-olds. Marie loved to watch him, too."

But it was Mac's education that was vitally important to Marie and Buddy. While he was at South Boston Catholic Academy through grade eight, Mac earned many scholarships but Marie managed to pay the remaining $1,000 through her three jobs. His four years at Catholic Memorial High School cost about $14,000 a year, but after scholarships, Mac's yearly tuition was $5,000, which Buddy gladly paid.

All Marie knew for sure after Tommy's death was

that this was not the time for her to die. "After Melissa's death, I just begged that I could stay alive long enough to see Mac graduate from high school," she said. "And I did. Now I want to see him graduate from college. I would give everything I could possibly have to see Melissa and Tommy one more time. So often I actually feel Tommy hugging me. And I dream about him and Melissa every single night. The pain is something I cannot put into words. It's more than just my heart that's aching. But I have to believe that everything happens in this world for a reason, one we may not understand. When I even mention my dying, Buddy tells me I can't die. That if I do a huge part of him will die as well. So, for Mac and for Buddy, I'm sticking around."

For two years after Tommy's death, Marie struggled to prove that she had no intention of leaving Mac and Buddy. Sadly, however, her health continued to deteriorate, providing one instance after another that her end was near. But Marie still insisted on living, no matter what her doctors said.

Everyone around her knew she was suffering physically, but her spirit seemed to soar, never losing its ability to laugh and see the very best in life. Although she was constantly moving from one hospital to one rehabilitation center, whatever room she was occupying was filled with family and friends who visited daily, bringing flowers, food, cards, and, most importantly, good jokes. But the Marie they visited was never lying in bed, meek and ill. Instead, she was offering her constant barrage of ribald jokes. Making fun of everything and everyone that

131

entered her room, she never hesitated to swear or relate a hilarious story.

"I'm not going to die today," she often pronounced to visitors, and they would, as her sister Jean admits, leave believing her and feeling better.

Susan, another of Marie's limitless visitors, looked forward to every moment she got to spend with her dear friend. "A few months ago, I received yet another call that Marie was desperately ill and had been read her last rites," Susan says. "I rushed to be by her side, and found her intubated and unable to speak. But when she heard my voice, she squeezed my hand and offered a weak smile. Heartbroken and in tears, I left the room certain that was the last time I would see my precious Marie. But, lo and behold, yet again, I was awakened in the morning by a call from Buddy that Marie had survived the night and would soon be heading to rehab. When I got to the rehab two days later, there she was, sitting in her bed, her nails and toenails freshly painted, wearing a beautiful blue dress and bright yellow sweater, welcoming me to come sit. Of course, she was making fun of someone, and complaining about the help, how no one there spoke English, and the food sucked. I knew then she was back to herself."

A few months later, Marie's friends were called to Tufts Medical Center in Boston at 9:30 pm and warned that she was even more dangerously ill than ever before. Again, Susan raced to the hospital where she met many friends and relatives who had also arrived to bid farewell to Marie. "As we rode on the elevator to the intensive care floor, we laughed and cried, frightened of what we were going to see, selfishly wanting her to stay alive, yet knowing how much she suffered," Susan says.

Outside Marie's room, the conversation on whether to resuscitate her grew heated. Buddy, wanting to keep Marie alive, spoke lovingly and hopefully while both her daughter Marie and sister Jean insisted Marie had suffered enough and would never want to exist with no decent quality of life. Tension and sadness filled the room as her closest friends and family gathered around Marie once again, this time her hands in restraints, so she would not pull out the breathing tube.

When Marie opened her eyes, everyone could see how much she wanted to speak. "She looked so frightened," Susan says. "I whispered that I loved her and told her I was pregnant. She squeezed my hand so tightly. I placed a scapular in her hand, and let the next family member have time with her."

Buddy stood at the foot of her bed, reassuring everyone that his beloved Marie would be well again. Then he reached into his shirt pocket and pulled out the most recent letters Mac, then a student at Santa Barbara Community College, had written and read it to her. While Mac had written them letters even before he went to Bridgewater State College, this one was written in November 2016, as it turned out, just a few short months before Marie died.

Dear Buddy and Nanna,

I hope all is well with the both of you. I can picture both of you sitting at the kitchen table and yelling back and forth because both of you are deaf as can be. I miss both of you like crazy. Before I continue, Nanna, no crying just smiles,

I am in a coffee shop now drinking tea and eating a piece of homemade cake. Although I miss Boston and you guys, I feel like I've grown up a lot. The people are different but that's not a bad thing. I get to experience new thinking and cultures. I also learned how much food I eat and how expensive it is. Most importantly how lucky I am to have been raised by the two best people in the world. I want to kill my roommates sometimes because I'm used to being alone or in a quiet house with just you two guys.

I miss your food, Nanna, and Buddy singing all morning as I am being grumpy in the morning. I miss Nanna telling me to be quiet and Buddy watching out the window waiting for someone to dare touch his car in the snowstorms. Seriously, I could not be more grateful for the life and opportunities you guys have given me. I hope we have many more years together even though I am here. I cannot wait to see you guys for Christmas....

When you guys are sitting at the table bored because I am not running up and down the stairs yelling about something, just know I am

*thinking about you guys every day and that I
can't wait to see you both.*

 *Anyway, stay healthy and sharp for me and
Nanna no crying just smiling. I love you guys
see you soon*

Love, Mackennan

In a school essay when he was in the 8th grade and applying to Catholic Memorial High School, Mac chose to write the following essay about his grandmother:

 *"In my eyes my grandmother is the best thing
that ever happened to me and the most important
person in my life. When I was three she took me
in (in actuality, Mac lived with Marie from the
day he returned home from the hospital). I will
never forget that. I haven't left since. When I
was three she managed to find the time to work
three jobs, morning, noon and night. She never
stopped. When she was at work, you could bet
I would be right there beside her. Her working
those three jobs paid my education fees my whole
life. She taught me responsibility that's key in life.
I learned that very quickly living with a single
grandmother.*

 *"My grandmother took me in. She did not
have to which meant no retirement, the rest of her
life was bringing me up. To me, most sixty-eight
year-olds are retired in Florida with palm trees.*

Not her, she is home making sure I eat, study, and go to bed early. She showed me love and loyalty to your family. Whenever I want to give up or have satisfactory work she pushes me to do my best. She took care of me for about ten years and all she asks back from me was to do good in school. If it wasn't for her I do not know where I would be or if I would be doing well in school. And I don't know if I would be applying to Catholic Memorial but I am because of her. When I grow up, I wish I am half the person my grandmother is. Now I know why they call her GRANDmother."

There are more letters written over the years, thanking Marie and Buddy for all the love, kindness and support that each had given him as he had grown up. He had also written how hard it had been to live through his mother's addiction and imprisonment and murder, and how he would never have survived without the two of them by his side. Mac was especially grateful to Buddy for teaching him sports. Buddy has saved every one of those letters for Mac is the love of his life, as was Marie.

Yet again, after hearing her adored grandson's most recent letter from California, where he was attending school, Marie was not ready to leave these two men she adored. "Wouldn't you know it, Marie pulled through once again, and was soon back at the rehab," Jean, who visited her sister constantly, says. "She was waiting for her coffee and donut from Buddy and making fun of someone who can't speak English or complaining about the lousy food. That's Marie in a nutshell, tough as nails when she needed to be, but soft as a lamb in her huge heart."

Ultimately and unsurprisingly, Marie lost the battle that she had fought so valiantly for so many years. On Wednesday, January 18, 2017, at 8:20 a.m., surrounded by her loved ones, Buddy, Jean Maggio, Butch, and her son Jimmy, she passed peacefully. She had her nails manicured red the day before she passed and her skin was silky smooth. "That's what my mom would want," her daughter Marie said.

Even though Marie had been very ill for years, and those who loved her knew the end was inevitable, all of them still confirmed that her passing deeply hurt, a fact proven by the tears shed at O'Brien's funeral home in Southie where, like her daughter Melissa four years earlier, Marie Falcione Hardy was waked. Again, the funeral home was packed with family and friends and beautiful floral arrangements. Marie's friends and former co-workers formed several different huddles, as each person appeared to have a memory to share, memories that often created laughter along with tears. Everyone there knew that Marie loved to make people laugh and, in her honor, the laughter never stopped that day and evening.

Her loving partner for thirty-five beautiful years, Buddy, stood very close to her casket, never leaving her side in death the way he had refused to do in life, reminding all who came to pay respects that Marie had fought a good fight.

At the wake, a woman took out a Mickey Mouse

watch with worn and ragged bands, tears in her eyes as she remembered the kindness Marie showed her scared little boy. She explained that Marie had given the watch to her son when he was in preschool, to try to comfort him and show him where the watch's hands should be when his mom would return. That little boy was now in his thirties, but he has never forgotten "the nice watch lady" who had made his days at Head Start special and loving.

She was that and more to her beloved Southie. Buddy puts it aptly when he says, "If we walked up Broadway, Marie would get hellos by twenty people at a time who would either say, 'There goes the teacher lady from the school or there goes the pizza lady from the hockey rink.'"

6. HER MOTHER'S DAUGHTER

THE NANCY YOUNG STORY

"Grief is the price of love," says Nancy Young, repeating a life lesson she not only learned the hard way, but inherited from a long line of family members' emotional traumas. Breaking the cycle of dysfunction and demons had always been Nancy's priority, but despite distancing herself from the suicide and addiction that afflicted all the men in her life—her father, her brother, the love of her life—and starting over in a new house, another life lesson emerged; you can run, but you can't hide.

After her niece Melissa found her own boyfriend hanging from the inside of a closet, leaving behind the traumatized, pregnant, single mother of a toddler, Nancy did everything to repress the trauma of her own Southie upbringing while holding together the blessings of the town she still calls home.

"Every man I ever loved hurt me by dying through suicide or drugs, breaking my heart and my soul, leaving me holding the ashes," Nancy says, "And the killer of my adored sister Karen was destroyed by alcohol abuse. But I'm still standing. And life is so worth living." *Life is worth living* is only one lesson passed down from her mother Flo. Like all the Southie women profiled in this book, harsh lessons of love and loss but especially of irrepressible resilience have been passed down from one generation to the next, as Nancy's story proves. She describes her own mother Flo as an angel in her life and in the life of others.

"I will miss her every day of my life," the fifty-five-year-old Nancy pours out, as if the loss is still raw and not more than twelve years old. And while not a mother herself, the never-married, proud aunt of Melissa has dedicated the rest of her life to family and to making damn sure the sins of the fathers will cease catching up with the children. She says she will do this by remembering where she came from.

While her story is powerful and inspirational enough to stand on its own, Nancy, an attractive, five-foot-five, blue-eyed blonde, considers her mother Flo inexorably tied to every aspect of the person she is today. Flo Young's resume is astounding, evidence of a Southie woman who believed she could change the world for the better and did everything within her power to do that. In the '70s, '80s, and '90s, Flo Young worked unremittingly for Head Start as a family service worker, a position similar to that of a social worker, sans the degree. Her job was to arrange screenings and medical appointments for low-income families, who were often her South Boston neighbors, but that was just a minuscule part of how Flo viewed her role with Head Start. Nancy knew that her mother adored every child that came through the program. One of Flo's co-workers told Nancy that a red dot on a child's file indicated the child was a priority to get into the program. All of Flo's files had red dots on them.

"My mother saw the good in everyone or always found an excuse or reason for the troubled," Nancy says. When Flo died, Nancy received many letters about her mother's work. A letter from Diana, one of Flo's mother's numerous single Head Start mothers, described how Flo, who introduced her to a prayer group, had saved her life. Diana also told Nancy that Flo especially adored the children who were a handful, the ones "who were off the walls." The teachers would be struggling to figure out how to handle the impossibly challenging child and Flo would say, "Oh the poor thing," or "What a darling!" Since Diana's family was not involved in her life, Flo became her family, genuinely caring about Diana and her children, taking them shopping, to the grocery store, to museums, to doctors' appointments, to the beach—always bringing along packed lunches. Flo even managed to help Diana find a much-needed job at Head Start, after which Diana continued her education and became a lead teacher, ultimately climbing the ranks to educational supervisor. Their relationship evolved into a beautiful friendship that Flo treasured.

Nancy understood that her mother's work wasn't complete until she had done all she could to help each young mother who lived in the South Boston housing projects. Flo was proud of the fact that when she was raising her own family there, these projects were a close-knit community.

"Everyone knew one another and helped in times of struggles," Nancy says. Proof of the power and resiliency of the projects can be seen in the fact that many residents chose to remain there, even after enduring the tragedies and hardships that some encountered.

"We certainly lived in the poorest part of town but we all felt a sense of pride that was shared by all us Lower Ender's," Nancy says. "Maybe some of our sense of pride came from all of Southie's great sports teams, but mostly it was the lifelong bonds our moms created for us."

Always having kids to hang out with was a huge gift for Nancy. As was the fact there was so much to keep her and her friends busy, including the park where she played softball, the concerts at the stadium, ice skating, and the beach. Kids never had to rely on their parents to be chauffeurs because everything was accessible. "I believe that is still true as evidenced by the influx of people currently moving into the community," Nancy says. "It's still an incredible place to live with plenty of remarkable people."

Yet, Nancy also vividly remembers the TPF (Tactical Police Force) in full riot gear on top of the roofs of their buildings during busing in the early '70's. "We would go over to Carson Beach and the mounted police were all lined up with white people on one side and the black people on the other side of the horses," Nancy says. "It was crazy and hostile. Such a sad time for our city."

Nancy never went to public school. Her parents sent all six of their children to Catholic schools from first to eighth grades, and allowed them to pick the high school of their choice. Because of busing, Nancy chose to stay in Catholic high school and attended Monsignor Ryan

Memorial. "I was fortunate not to have to be afraid at school, but I do remember one of my neighbors, Michael, being the first to get stabbed by another student," Nancy says. "It was scary listening to your parents talking about all of this. If my mother could have fixed that horrific situation, she surely would have. But she had to admit there was nothing even she could do."

It hadn't been until Louise Day Hicks became elected to the Boston School Committee that Southie women got involved in politics. Once they did, like Elaine Sweeney McGuire, they were tenacious. Forced busing proved how far Southie women would go to protect their children. Nancy and her friends viewed their mothers as the backbones of their lives and of their communities. "They saw the strength they had and the power and it changed everything," Nancy says.

Sadly, the safety and well-being that Flo worked to bestow on all her clients in no way extended to her own life. Tragedy knocked at Flo's door far too many times, but, somehow, she endured and still struggled to do what she could to help others. Above all else, Flo was the mother who, while dedicating herself to those less fortunate, never considered anything more important than her own family—a family wracked by pain and suffering.

"I was always taught that God will only give to you what you can handle," Nancy says. "I have questioned my faith many times but find myself in crisis looking to God. I have many times silently thought, *Why my family?* but then answered, *Why not?* Why should I say that someone else should suffer to spare my pain?"

The Good, the Bad, and the Worst

Her fondest memories came from her childhood spent in the Old Colony housing projects. "You might say we all put the word *fun* in dysfunction, and I mean that to be a compliment," she says. "You would walk out the door and there was always someone to hang out with. We had a huge park across the street and beach across from the park."

Nancy finds it interesting that for all the adversity her town has endured over the years that people are now spending excessive amounts of money to move there. She considers South Boston as she once knew it, obsolete. "Now when I go up Castle Island, or down Broadway, I don't know anybody. In my time, you knew everyone and I mean everyone."

It comes as no surprise that Nancy recently renovated the third floor of her two-family home to make a spacious apartment for herself and her brother Charlie. Her thirty-one-year-old nephew lives one floor beneath her. On the first floor of the house, her brother Joseph lives with his girlfriend Amanda and their eight-year-old son Ronan, a high functioning autistic child. "Ronan is a joy, so sweet and innocent," Nancy says. "We all adore him."

Nancy speaks equally lovingly and proudly of all the relatives who live in her house, especially her two younger brothers, Charlie who is fifty-two, and Joseph, fifty. "My brothers are very close to one another," Nancy says. "They are very loyal to each other. Charlie is extremely intelligent. He loves history, and I'm always floored at his knowledge of politics, other countries, and current events. We'll watch *Jeopardy* and he amazingly yells out every correct answer. He reminds me a lot of my father.

"Joseph is more on the private side and has a lot of my mother's personality. He's much more humble than any of us, a lot like my brother Michael. Joseph was the one who suffered mentally and emotionally from our family's trials and tribulations more than any of us."

For five years, Charlie lived in Ireland with his wife, Denise, from whom he is now divorced. Their one child, Christopher, was born there. Charlie has been a truck driver for years, and, recently, Joseph, a former drug counselor and the father of Melissa, found gainful employment at the company where Charlie works.

Nancy's two brothers are recovering heroin addicts, both of whom started to do heroin in their early thirties. Nancy would never place any of the fault of their problems on the place where they grew up.

"They were grown men who made that choice to stick a needle into their arm," Nancy says. "Truthfully, I do not know if they will ever be totally drug free. Today is going good for them but I do not know what tomorrow will bring. They say relapse is part of recovery and that has happened. Of course, there is a possibility of one of them overdosing if they relapse and all the worrying in the world will not change that. You cannot babysit them. You can only hope and pray that they see the light. I do not want to say it is a drug you cannot ever get away from because I have seen firsthand some great success stories. It is like anything in life. You have to really want it. Success is hard work, as is recovery. The AA motto 'Nothing changes if nothing changes' sums it up. As far as worrying about them goes, I have come to the realization that this is their journey. I have wasted far too much energy focusing on the lives of others and their behaviors to which I have no control. *Que sera, sera.* I will endure what the future holds for me and pray for my brothers that they have the strength to keep fighting the demons within."

Nancy admits that some might think it strange that she lives in her house along with so many members of her extended family, but she is perfectly satisfied with the situation. Her brothers do snow removal and lots of other jobs around the house. Also, in her job at Eversource, New England's largest energy delivery service, where she has worked for the past 32 years, Nancy works long hours and is not home a lot. "Oh, sure, every once in a while, I go, 'Oh, My God!'" she says. "But I know I would be bored if they weren't all here with me."

Nancy is proud that like her mother, she maintains this deep love for and devotion to family. While horrific tragedies befell the Young family, Nancy remains grateful for the unique pleasures that life in a family with five siblings and an adoring mother brought to her childhood.

And while pain arrived on far too many of those days, Nancy will never forget the years of warmth and laughter, the joyfulness of being Flo's daughter during those early years. While Nancy's father, Joseph, was an only child, her mother, one of eight children, three girls and five boys, knew what it was like to grow up in an outsized family. As a result Nancy grew up surrounded by her mother's family, which included twenty-seven first cousins, fourteen of whom lived in nearby Weymouth.

"We were lucky kids seeing as my aunt lived so close to the beach and so did we," she says. "Much of our younger years were on the ocean. My mother would pack lunches and we would all pile into in her station wagon with the paneling on the side for a fun filled day at Carson Beach in South Boston. My mother's friends would be over there with their children and we would make sand castles, play with our shovels and pails and just run around and cool off in the ocean. Nothing quite like the serenity of the ocean. We were always on the go."

Nancy's brothers, especially Charlie, were excellent hockey players and on traveling teams, so, in the winter, the family would travel to different skating rinks watching them play hockey. "My mother would also drop us off for public skating and pick us up when it was over, and as we got older we hopped on the bus," Nancy says. "Kids from all over the town went to the rink for public skating, and it was so much fun."

In the summer, Flo signed up her children for a camp program at Boston University. The bus would pick them up at St. Monica's church for their fun-filled day at camp. Kids from all over the city would be bussed to BU to compete in track and field, swimming, sprinting, etc. "We were so fortunate," Nancy says. "Our parents allowed us a life full of happy childhood memories with family and friends. You can't help but wonder how and why things turned out the way they did."

Although Nancy has never managed to find the answer to that painful question, she knows that her mother's legacy, despite all she gave to others in need, will always be the importance of family. Today, for Nancy, everything, all the joy and all the pain, still revolves around her family. And it was within her family that Nancy first found the beginnings of the pain that would fill so many of her future days.

When Nancy was sixteen, her father had left his job as a teamster for Local 25 where he had worked for twenty-five years, but he never shared why that happened with anyone in the household. Flo had minimal income from her job, and Nancy, Charlie, and Joseph were still dependent upon her. When Flo had to make a tough choice to get some financial assistance, her husband was devastated, insisting his family would never go on welfare. All Flo could answer was, "Joe, what am I supposed to do?"

Nancy was already paying to finish high school. Karen and Michael, both lived on their own and were working full time. Yet they did all they could to help their younger siblings, Joseph, Charlie, and Nancy, who along with Tinka who was working, were living together at home. Hard as it was for Joe to accept, there was no other choice.

It wasn't too soon after that Flo suffered two nervous breakdowns. When Flo had finally confided in Karen that she was struggling mentally, her oldest daughter brought her to New England Medical where she was sent to Glenside, a psychiatric facility for adults. "When Tinka came home to tell our father that Flo had been admitted to Glenside, he cried his eyes out," Nancy says. She hated the fact that while Flo was at Glenside, her mother was heavily sedated. Years later, Nancy asked Flo how she had known she was having a breakdown. "She told me she could not collect her thoughts or sleep, lost weight, cried a lot, and was deeply depressed," Nancy says.

Since income was minimal during that time, Nancy contributed by working at the nearby Teen Center and helping to pay for her last two years of private high school. "My father was a great cook so it was just cleaning and helping with shopping and laundry," Nancy says. "Of course, we missed our mother terribly. At that time, I had no idea what a breakdown was."

After some time, Flo became an outpatient and all the members of the Young family attended family meetings at New England Medical Center. "Boy, can those be treacherous when we were airing out the feelings we all had for another," Nancy says. Eventually, family members simply stopped going.

Nancy finds one silver lining in her mother's time at Glenside; in particular, her mother's roommate who also worked for Head Start, but in a different area. Kate, like Flo, had six children. The two women had a great deal in common and became close friends for years to come, frequently meeting for lunch in Chinatown to catch up on their lives.

"The reason they didn't interact elsewhere was that Kate was black and my mother was white," Nancy says. "Racial tensions were pretty heated in our neighborhoods, and neither woman wanted to jeopardize the other."

Nancy feels that part of her mother's problems was related to the fact that she kept everything inside. Nancy insists she is more like her father, direct and open, and lacking in her mother's patience. "I have a very strong personality and make my feelings known," Nancy says. "I just wish my mother had been able to do the same during that difficult time."

It was after Flo left Glenside and was receiving therapy as an outpatient when the first of far too many tragedies struck this one family. Nancy was only seventeen, a few months shy of her eighteenth birthday. It was a freezing cold, icy February evening and her friend Barbie had come over to listen to music when they noticed a speaker was missing. "I looked around the house and didn't see my father," Nancy remembers.

Where he would've been sitting in his regular spot in the living room, Nancy only saw her father's glasses. She smelled a lingering scent of his cologne. He had obviously been close by. When she looked at the bedroom to the left, she saw the speaker wire wrapped around the door. Instantly, she sensed something was wrong.

"I ran to the door of the bedroom and turned on the light and it would not turn on," she says. "I could feel something heavy as I pushed the door but it was dark and it was nighttime. I could not quite see but I knew from the shadow what I was witnessing. I have no idea how I knew, but I just did. My heart was barely beating and I was sure I would collapse, but I just knew from that dark shadow. My father had hanged himself."

Nancy knew her mother would be returning soon

from her prayer group, and she couldn't think of anything, except that her mother should not see what she knew was the hideous shadow behind the door. She could not see in the room because her father had removed the light bulb, but she knew there was no way she could cut him down by herself.

"That's all I was thinking," Nancy says. "Cut him down. Cut him down. Maybe it wasn't too late." Nancy found her sister Karen who, along with a neighbor, Willy, got her father down. Another neighbor, Maureen Weeks, who was a nurse, applied CPR but to no avail.

Nancy remembers being out front when the EMTs carried her father out. She was next to the ambulance, and when she looked in the car window, she saw him again. "His head was thick and swollen to twice its normal size and his face had turned blue," she says. "I will never forget that hideous sight. It was all a nightmare. My siblings were a mess. We were totally traumatized. It was horrifying."

Nancy managed to repress this memory for many years but eventually she was no longer able to do so. "Things will resurface whether you like it or not," she says. And to know her own niece Melissa would suffer the same trauma pains Nancy beyond belief.

"I try not to think about it because after all these years, it is still very raw," Nancy says. "When I do think about it, I am as emotional as the day it happened. I struggle with it. I do not share the same opinion that others have that suicide is a coward's way out because I think it takes a great deal of courage to basically murder yourself. In my mind, suicide is the hardest death ever. It is so hard for me to imagine not wanting to live and fight for your life."

Many years after her father died, one of his fellow workers' son told Nancy that he thought Joe had quit his job as a hard working truck driver because he had feared he was going blind. "Maybe he thought he was being noble by sparing us the truth," Nancy says. "I will never know. We all knew he was depressed, especially with what was going on with my mother, but no one could have ever imagined he would take his own life."

It took many years for Nancy to forgive her father. All she wanted to know was why would he do this? Especially since her poor mother was in outpatient care for her recent breakdown, struggling to get well. *How could he do this to her, of all people?*

"After this, my mom was completely distraught and just a complete mess for a long time," Nancy says. "I was in my last year of high school, and I now had a father who'd killed himself and a mother who was struggling with severe depression. Me and Tinka, who were still living at home, had no choice but to try to get over our own sorrow and care for Charlie and Joseph and do all we could to help our mother heal. She was all we had now and we loved her so much."

Nancy remembers the pure fright in her mother's eyes and her crying, "How am I going to take care of you guys?" Neighbors were overwhelmingly supportive, supplying endless amounts of food, company, and comfort before and continuously after the funeral services, but the problems within the Young house continued to mount.

One day, desperate to have her mother back and infuriated at seeing what her father's death was doing to her, Nancy took her mother by her shoulders and said, "Look at you, Ma. What's more important, his death or your life? We cannot go on like this any longer. I'm way too young to be trying to help my brothers deal with our dysfunction. I need my mother and I need her now."

Two days after her father died on February 4th, Nancy found a note that was dated just a week earlier. "I cannot fathom that he planned his death," Nancy says. "As years go on and I read articles in the newspaper I say, 'Thank you, God, that he only did it to himself and not to the rest of us.' I ask myself why he did not reach out for help. It was not on impulse. It was a planned death."

Nancy will never share the contents of that note, insistent on maintaining some privacy. Her father's words were meant only for his family. "He deserves that much respect," Nancy says "As it is, I know some people will hate that I resurrected all this. But my life is my life and I know my history and I am not ashamed of it. Do I wish things were different? Absolutely, but they are not. And if by telling our story, I can help one person know there is life after suicide, and forgiveness, then it was not in vain."

For many years after her father's death, Nancy could not lessen her resentment of how her father had damaged her mother. "He knew how wounded she was, and I thought he was so mean to leave her like that," Nancy says. "Maybe my anger was just a defense mechanism for me to not have to deal with his suicide."

Still, looking at her mother after her father died, Nancy knew that she never wanted to feel that hopeless. "In reality, after that day, every man I ever loved hurt me," Nancy says. "My father, and, later, Mark, the love of my life, my brother, and my sister Karen's boyfriend, Jackie. Of all of them, my father was the one who was supposed to protect me. I was his baby girl. Instead, he scarred me the most. I'm sure it was not his intention, but it is my reality. That could have been one of the reasons I did not marry. But I was far from the only one scarred by his death. We were all lost at that time."

Somehow, Flo Young managed to overcome her own fragility, and pull herself and her shattered family together, miraculously becoming a stronger and wiser woman, continuing her life's work of helping other families through their difficult times, making sure their children received the help they needed and deserved.

"Through all this pain and uncertainty, my mother was and will always continue to be the wind beneath my wings," Nancy says. "She taught me so many lessons from her heartache. In so many ways, I wanted to be like my mother and in so many other ways I did not. I loved her love of life, her compassion for people, and the drive she instilled in me. She made me realize through her limitations the importance of education and independence, as well as the bond of a family. I think she pushed me the most because she knew I had what it took. I loved to learn, and if I said I was going to do something, I did it. I have always been strong willed. I did not like that my mother could easily be taken for granted. It ate at me that people often took her kindness for weakness. She never gave herself enough credit for all she did."

Nancy was grateful that her adored grandfather was no longer living when his son took his own life in the house in which they all lived together. One of the greatest pleasures of her childhood had been the fact that her father's father, who was also named Joseph but called Pop Pop, had moved into their house in 1959, three years before she was born, after his wife died of breast cancer. The apartment was very crowded, with three brothers sharing one bedroom and the three sisters sharing another. Nancy's parents slept on a pullout couch in the living room. Because they were considered under-housed, ultimately, they were able to apply for a larger unit in the projects. When the apartment next door finally became vacant, the housing authority broke through the wall, giving the Young family three additional rooms and an additional bathroom, referring to that new area as the breakthrough. "It was a brilliant and much-needed change," Nancy says.

Nancy adored her grandfather, a kind, gentle man who loved to draw nature pictures and spend time with his grandchildren. He suffered with his breathing from years of smoking, necessitating a breathing machine in his room. Since Nancy's father had been an only child, Nancy and her siblings were Pop Pop's only grandchildren. "He was so kind to all of us," Nancy says. "He was the perfect picture of a grandfather, a wonderful male role model. It was like having two fathers, only one spoiled us and the real one was the disciplinarian. Pop Pop passed away when I was fourteen. I was heartbroken."

Though the family, thanks to Flo's miraculous strength, survived the nightmare of losing Nancy's father, Nancy will always be tortured by the way he died. "You just never know why suicide happens and always wonder what you might have done to have caused it and what you might have been able to do to prevent it. I cannot stop thinking how lonely he must have felt. If only he could have confided in one of us. I hope he has found peace."

It was years later that Nancy finally went into therapy, and understood that she was suffering from post traumatic stress from her father's death. But that was not the only traumatic stress that Nancy and her family would suffer. Though this one was not caused, Nancy emphasizes, by someone wanting to die.

This tragedy occurred when Karen Young, the oldest of Flo's six children, was strangled by her boyfriend, Jackie, on January 25th, 1985, five years after their father had died. Nancy will never forget the day of the murder, any more than she can forget the day her father died.

"I was sitting home and I got a phone call from a friend whose building was connected to my sister's," she says. "He told me there were firefighters and cops at Karen's house. All I could think was, *feet don't fail me now.*"

When Nancy got to the second floor landing, officer Jack McGill would not let her go in. When he told her he believed her sister was dead, Nancy slid all the way down the hallway wall, crying out, "My poor mother!"

When Flo arrived, mother and daughter stood in front of the building, holding each other up, as the police finally walked out of Karen's apartment with her boyfriend Jackie in handcuffs. Jackie had made the call to the police telling them he just killed someone.

Karen had been a secretary at the Intensive Care Unit at Boston City Hospital, the same hospital where she was taken after the incident. "When we were allowed to see her," Nancy remembers, "she was wrapped in a very cold blanket because her temperature was 107. The blood vessels on the side of her face were all broken. The doctor told me that everywhere in the hospital people were talking about her in disbelief because they all really loved her. Because she had a slight pulse they had to do two brain scans twenty-four hours apart so that they could say for sure the strangulation was the cause of death."

Karen Young was declared dead on January 27, 1985, at the age of twenty-nine. More than thirty years later, Nancy can still picture her sister standing in front of her, her pretty face and vibrant smile, her straight brown hair always parted in the middle. "She had just the perfect shape, not too thin, never overweight," Nancy says. "And such an outgoing personality, always so confident and independent and hard working, and a fierce protector of her three younger brothers and two younger sisters. I often think of what we could have accomplished together if she had not died. To this day people will sometimes say to me, 'Hi, Karen,' and then say, 'Oh, I mean Nancy.' To me that is such a compliment to think that she is still thought of after all these years. She was just the perfect sister and there is not a day that goes by that I do not miss her."

As hideous and shocking as the murder was, it is what Nancy adds about the murder that is even more astonishing, as well as one more example of the unique strength and beauty of both Flo and her daughter. Heartbroken though the Young family was to lose Karen, their hearts also went out to Jackie's family, who they felt were suffering as much as they were.

"Jackie's brother came to my home and extended his condolences and even offered to pay for the funeral services," Nancy says. "You could see the pain etched on his face. My mother never blamed anyone but Jackie for what happened to Karen. His father, brothers, and one sister came to pay their respects at the wake, something I always admired."

Once again, the Young family received endless supplies of food, company, and support. "It affected everyone as if we were one big family," Nancy says.

After Karen's tragic death, Flo and Nancy and the rest of the family did what they always did; they put one foot in front of the other and moved forward. But Nancy witnessed the devastation her sister's death caused her mother and grieved as deeply for her mother's loss as she did for her own.

"I saw how my family struggled with all its tragedies," Nancy says. "Some of us self-medicated while others strove to just survive. When my brothers went to therapy, they were prescribed legal meds, which they started abusing. They loved downers like Valium and Klonopin, and with all their suffering, I can see why a doctor would prescribe them."

Things got even worse for Charlie when, at eighteen, he was in a motorcycle accident in which he sustained an open compound fracture on his ankle, causing chronic pain he often controlled with prescription drugs.

Even though there was so much pain in their lives, thanks to Flo, who would not surrender to her second horrendous grief, the family still experienced many good times. "She was truly inspiring, for she loved life so much, especially children," Nancy says. "I think she adored the innocence of them, so pure and naive. And through everything that happened to her, she kept her faith. She went to prayer groups at St. Augustine's and found great comfort within its members."

A support group called Omega was especially important in Flo's life after her two tragic losses. Many years later, Nancy found a letter that her mother had written expressing her feelings for this group.

"The minute I learned of my husband's death, I became engaged in my own life-and-death struggle. Despite an agony that must have approached his own pain I could not make that decision he made. Omega taught me it is okay to be afraid of things we don't understand. It's okay to think, worry, and cry. That eventually you're going to adjust to changes life brings your way and you'll soon realize that it is okay to love again and laugh again and it will be that way because you made it that way. I have also learned not to let the nightmare of those two nights take away the love we had as a family. I will always cry because my children and I are deprived of the sight and

sound of Joe and Karen. We were blessed because they were ours. Their memories will help mend our broken hearts."

Flo also found solace as a subscriber of POMC, Parents of Murdered Children. The quarterly newsletters this nonprofit group sent made her realize she was not alone. POMC has a traveling wall where those who lost loved ones can put those names on a plaque, which is then added to the wall. Every year, POMC sends a card on the anniversary of Karen's death.

"We all loved one another, and we were never shy to let each other know that," Nancy says. "I never left my house without kissing my mother goodbye. She raised us all to be very loving and caring."

Ironically, years later when Flo was dying and Nancy was struggling to find her a room at the completely occupied Marian Manor nursing home in Southie, Jackie's sister, who worked there, came forward to help. "As soon as I saw your mother's name on the waiting list, I knew we had to get her in," she told Nancy, somehow managing to secure a private room for Flo, proving to Nancy and to Flo that the good in the world manages to trump the bad.

The Mark of Love

Soon after Karen's death, Nancy, who was twenty-three at the time, began a special relationship with twenty-six-year-old Mark Estes. She knew about his past, the seven years he had spent in jail at a young age, and felt he had paid his debt to society. Almost from that beginning of his release, he became a crucial part of Nancy's life.

"I loved him very much," she says. "He loved me back and it was all so special. But I was so sure, like so many other women who love men who have had trouble in their lives, that things would be different with us. He was so full of life, always living life for the moment."

A handsome kid who worked construction, Mark was the life of the party and totally charming. "He taught me things that we all took for granted," Nancy says. "For example, he loved watching the birds and sitting up at Castle Island, especially when it rained, simply looking at the water and smelling the ocean. He was mesmerized by the ocean. And he loved getting suntanned. 'These are the things,' he would tell me, 'that you miss when you are incarcerated.'"

For the most part, Nancy and Mark lived simply, going to movies, out to dinner, or for walks. "The thing I loved most about Mark was that he totally embraced life," Nancy says. "He had so much energy and was always in a good mood. He had the ability to put a smile on peoples' faces. He was just fun to be around."

The two of them especially enjoyed traveling together, heading to Ireland for Nancy's brother Charlie's wedding, as well as to Venice and London. In London, they went to the original Hard Rock Cafe, walked through Piccadilly Park, and traveled the underground subway all over the city. "In Venice, like typical tourists, we fed the birds at St. Mark's Square, took a gondola ride, and found Marco

Polo's house near the Rialto Bridge and the Grand Canal," Nancy says.

Mark was fascinated by the architecture in Europe, always remarking on the craftsmanship, in awe of the fact that this work was done so many years ago, all by hand. He would stare at the gargoyles on the churches for hours, sights the two of them found breathtaking. They also visited Montreal and took several trips to California to visit Nancy's sister Tinka's family.

Mark and Nancy even bought a timeshare at the Vistana Resort on Lake Buena Vista in Orlando when they were in Florida. Here, they did everything together, visiting Disney World and Epcot, and traveling to Tampa to enjoy the rides and animals at Busch Gardens. Mark loved Pleasure Island in Downtown Orlando, insisting that every night was New Year's Eve there. "Mark had such a knack for being able to make you laugh even if you were angry," Nancy says. "He was always genuinely kind to the people he cared for."

Nancy found it interesting that Mark, with his jet-black hair and baby-blue eyes, resembled both her brother Michael and her father. "Mark was slighter in stature than my brother and father. I don't believe he weighed more than a hundred and fifty pounds," Nancy says. "He was slender and wore pants that were only a size thirty. He was so handsome. Of course, I cannot be impartial about that because I loved him, but there was no denying the fact that he was a good-looking guy. He was always personable and never mean. He had just headed down the wrong path."

Nancy loved the fact that Mark never took life too seriously, that he was always laughing and cracking jokes. "I adored his personality, his love of his family and how well read he was. He particularly favored Robert Ludlum, such as *The Bourne Supremacy,* and *The Bourne Ultimatum.* You could talk about anything with him."

It meant a lot to Nancy that her mother liked Mark. "Just like her, he enjoyed being with people," Nancy says. "When she saw him getting back into drugs and starting to party, of course, she was concerned for me. However, my mother always encouraged us to see things for ourselves. And she was never judgmental. Whatever made me happy was good for my mother as long as there was no abuse."

Nancy believed being incarcerated at such a young age changes a person. But she had hoped that by traveling with Mark and showing him so many of the finer things in life, it would encourage him to strive to want these things for himself. She was certain that Mark tried his best to be a good citizen. "But it was a struggle and when you add drugs to that equation, the result can never be good," she says. "Of course, I thought I could save Mark. He used to say how lucky he was to have met me. He would ask me, 'Nancy, do you think I like what I am doing?' But I learned, all too soon, that no one can ever compete with heroin. It will win every time. The individual has to want to give it up, and that doesn't often happen. I just wish I could have fixed him so we could have had a great life. If it had not been for the drugs, I think I would have married Mark. We talked often of getting married. I had a beautiful diamond, which I have to this day. He so wanted children but I knew that wasn't a good idea with what was going on in his life. It is all so sad because we had a great love affair."

Nancy considers the first six years of their relationship some of the best of her life. But when heroin entered their relationship, everything fractured. The change was gradual, but when the habit became more intense for him, nothing was the same for the two of them. Mark no longer wanted just to hang out or go for walks with her. He would nod off during a movie and Nancy would get angry. Their arguments became more frequent, and for the first time in six years, they began to break up. Mark tried several rehabs, but they didn't help. "He would come out feeling good and wanted to do the right thing but that drug is so damn powerful," Nancy says. "No one can compete with that drug, and I mean no one. All I would hear were lies, lies, and more lies. I was fighting a losing battle and felt so hopeless. Bear in my mind, all my brothers were on heroin as well. I still do not know how I stayed sane."

The longest Nancy and Mark stayed away from one another was five months, during which time he started dating someone else. Yet, he never lost contact with her and would call occasionally just to talk. So often, he would repeat, "Do you think I like what I became?" and they both knew the answer was no. But that didn't change the way he was.

Eventually Nancy and Mark got back together but things had changed. They still went out and did many of the things they used to do together, but underneath there were hard feelings, and, of course, there were still the drugs. "We each felt the difference in our relationship, but our mutual love for one another was not ready to die," Nancy says. She was crushed that everything they had accomplished as a couple was not enough to keep him away from his addiction. But she also understood, having witnessed this fact far too often, that you can easily become a product of your environment; in particular, the people he did drugs with.

"It is very easy for a person who is not in love with someone to think it is that much easier to leave someone you love, but my mother had always taught me to try and help the ones you love," Nancy says. "And I loved Mark so very much. But I couldn't keep him from making his bad choices. One of those bad choices ultimately cost him his life."

On June 12th, 1995, two weeks after Nancy and Mark returned from a trip to California, Mark Estes was murdered, just up the street from where Nancy lived. Like the two former hideous days in her life, every detail of that day is engraved permanently in her mind. Around one o'clock that morning, Nancy woke up to hear her mother talking on the phone to her brother Joseph, saying someone had been shot. "When she told me that Mark had just been shot, I raced to get dressed," Nancy says. "And when I reached the corner, Mark was lying motionless, with blood oozing out of his mouth, between the white lines the police had set up. My worst nightmare had come true. I knew right then and there that Mark was no longer with us."

When Nancy got to Boston City Hospital where Mark was transported, she was allowed to see him. He was intubated and a sheet and a blanket were pulled up to his neck, but to Nancy, surprisingly, he didn't look traumatized. Since the two had just returned from their visit to California two weeks earlier, he was still tanned. "I could not stop staring at that face, trying to block out everything else that had happened to Mark's body," Nancy says. "I had known from the moment I walked through the double doors that he had gotten shot multiple times. I had heard one of the hospital staff say, 'Oh, my God, who could have done this to someone?' Since Boston City Hospital sees so much trauma, this situation had to be really bad to affect the staff this way. My heart was totally broken. I could not imagine how I was going to tell his family and how on earth I was going to function."

After she left the hospital, barely able to move or think, Nancy somehow found her way first to Mark's brother's house to inform him of Mark's murder and then to the exact place where Mark had died. She was not certain why, but she felt an overwhelming need to be there. "Perhaps it was feeling close to him or maybe to see if his killer had left anything behind or maybe he would return, and I stood there, in that one spot, and cried my heart out," Nancy says. "Ten years of trying to help someone find his self worth and it ends with him in between the white line of a crosswalk where police set up yellow tape as a crime scene. I was numb. It was surreal."

Nancy finally went home in the early morning hours. Sleep, of course, was out the question for Nancy that night.

Or for many other nights. "My sister Karen, for obvious reasons, was front and center," Nancy says. "I now had two people I loved murdered." Deeply wounded, Nancy found herself unable to sit in one place for a long period of time. After one particular sleepless night, she got up and went to the convenience store, ending up walking around the projects in despair. There, she had a brief encounter with the person who was alleged to have killed Mark. "I told him he fucked up and he said, 'Is that so?' And I said, 'Yes, because I'm still here.' He got in my face and we were going back and forth with one another until one of my neighbors intervened and forced him to leave. I don't know what might have happened had the neighbor not appeared."

The newspaper stories about Mark's death presented yet another struggle for Nancy. Now she had to read about Mark's life being dissected in the media, with speculation on who'd killed him and why. For her, however, what was done was done and she was left to pick up the pieces of her life. She heard some people say, "She's better off," or "She deserved better," and while perhaps that was true, the fact remained that she loved Mark very much. "I knew things about him that they did not know that gave me a far better understanding of his bad choices," Nancy says. "And regardless of whether people felt I was better off or not, nothing could erase my heartache and the fact that I was now trying to cope with a third tragic loss."

Nancy understands only too well that the whole perception of the power of heroin addiction is different today than it was when Mark died, that people see it as an epidemic and are trying to deal with it as such. "Still, there is no hell quite like the hell of watching dope change somebody you love into somebody you don't even recognize," Nancy says. "I do not think I had a good night's sleep for at least six months. I had to talk to detectives, hear all the rumors, and try and sort my life back to a new normalcy, not that it ever was normal after that."

Nothing Changes If Nothing Changes

After those six months, Nancy finally began a slow healing process. Mark was no longer her first thought in the morning nor her last thought of the evening. Her main focus after he died was to move out of the projects. Working hard every opportunity she could, four years after Mark's death, she purchased her first home. When Nancy had begun working for Boston Edison, which became Eversource, she had first seen that it wasn't only wealthy people who owned homes. While she had loved living in the projects and could not have asked for a better group of people to live with, she felt she needed to change everything in her life and focus on the positive that life had to offer.

"I set out on a mission and I did it," she says. "It could have been easier to have a pity party for myself, but at the end of the day you are solely responsible for what your wants and needs are, and I wanted to be happy, to buy a house, and that was what I did."

To this day, Mark's murder has not been resolved. Nancy put his name on the POMC wall, as her mother did before her for her sister Karen. "I will never stop loving or missing Mark," she says. "I can only hope he has found peace."

Thirty-three at the time of Mark's death, Nancy felt wounds so deep she wondered how much more she could take. But Flo made sure Nancy always understood that life is for the living and, following her mother's lead yet again, Nancy moved on in her own life, reveling in the love of her family, her three brothers, Michael, Joseph, and Charlie, and her older sister Tinka, the only Young who had ever truly left Southie.

But tragedy was not quite through with the Young family, striking again in 2000, five years after Mark's death. This time it hit Michael, Nancy's older brother. Nancy lights up when she talks about Michael. To her, he was "the prodigal son," the one who did everything right. He was the altar boy, the shoeshine boy, the newspaper boy, and a terrific big brother. Right after high school he had enlisted in the Marines to please their father who could easily recite the Eleven General Orders of the Marine Corps. "My dad was a proud Marine and a true patriot," Nancy says. "I remember my sister was wearing a dungaree coat with the American flag on it. My dad damn near went through the roof, yelling, 'How dare you desecrate the American flag!'"

But Michael's attempt to please their father fell apart when he was in boot camp and severely injured his shin and was medically discharged. Over the next few years, he underwent multiple surgeries on this leg, yet nothing could relieve the pain that made him cry out every night or allow him to return to his normal life. The orthopedic surgeon implanted a device in his shin that was supposed to stretch the bone to fuse them together. When the device was tightened, however, Michael was in agony.

"It was heart wrenching to watch him suffer like this," Nancy says. He did get married in his twenties and had a son and a daughter, but was divorced years later. By the twentieth surgery on his leg, Michael had become dependent on pain drugs. Nancy watched helplessly as the strong older brother she loved, the man who worked for the post office and took all his duties seriously, became a legal junkie. And when those pain meds no longer worked, he resorted to heroin.

"You never, ever, and I mean never ever, want to experience your loved one on this drug," Nancy says. "It is the saddest of them all. One day I walked into the house and he had foam coming out of his mouth. Michael was in intensive care for ten days before he died. When we brought him into the hospital, he had global brain damage. He died from aspiration pneumonia. Basically, he swallowed his own vomit because he was so high. He was forty-one. Tragic, tragic, tragic. Another child my poor mother had to bury."

After Michael died, Nancy told her mother that nothing could be worse than a mother burying a child. But her mother surprised her, saying, "If your father didn't kill himself, I would feel that way. But Karen didn't choose to die and Michael's death was an accident. It was indescribably hideous to lose a child, but your father chose to die and that affected me horribly"

Once again, Nancy saw her mother struggling not to be crushed. This time, however, Flo's health had been compromised by several bouts of cancer, and she looked frail to Nancy. But still Flo continued to work the job she loved, finding the strength and the skills to help children and mothers in need. Nancy followed her mother's example. "I refused to let my life be defined by the tragedies I had experienced," Nancy says firmly. "I remembered that life is for the living."

Discussing the addiction problem in her own family is difficult for Nancy, but she has never been one to avoid the truth, no matter how painful it might be. Talking about Joseph's and Charlie's heroin addictions is agonizing but her two younger brothers' recovery attempts, along with her realistic view of the near impossibility of total recovery, fuel her desire to tell her family's story both honestly and lovingly.

Coming Clean about Junk

"Charlie's and Joseph's addictions to heroin began somewhere in their late twenties and early thirties," Nancy says. "Both of them lived outside the home with their wives so we were not aware until the addictions took their toll on their personal lives. Eventually, the marriages crumbled; rightfully so. We were on foreign ground with what heroin was all about, except that a junkie was the worst addict ever. And that my brothers were full-blown junkies. My mother was always supportive of her sons, but she was devastated. Who wouldn't be? It always mystified me how some members of families are polar opposites.

"But life with a heroin addict is pure hell. The countless times you would come home only to find one of my two brothers on the floor, call the ambulance, they revive them, take them to the hospital, and then they come out to do the same thing. It's a vicious cycle and incomprehensible. I couldn't fathom why someone would play Russian roulette with your life. My mother would say it was a disease, and me and Tinka would say they should get help. If you have cancer, you get treatment, so why wouldn't they? Then when they started treatment, they would stay clean for a little while and go right back to the bad behavior. Over time and the longer you stay in the game, you are sure to get arrested and that is exactly what happened. Eventually every one of my brothers ended up doing time as a result of heroin."

One day while Flo was being treated for cancer, Nancy dropped her off from her chemotherapy treatment and went to use her mother's bathroom. When she pushed her bathroom door, Charlie fell to the ground. He had tried to hang himself and when Nancy had pushed the door, he'd fallen. "He started crawling on the floor and I was like, 'What are you doing?'" Nancy says.

Nancy called the best team at the Boston Medical Center and after they evaluated him, Charlie was put in the Beth Israel Psychiatric Unit. "He was so skinny, like malnutrition skinny," Nancy says. "He'd left a note that he didn't want to live. Here was my poor mother battling breast cancer and now her son is hospitalized for trying to kill himself. Good Lord. It was never-ending.

"There were many times when you would ask God to spare my brothers of this life and please take them. I know it may sound harsh, especially from someone who has lost so much, but like I said, there is no hell like the hell of watching dope turn someone you love into someone you do not even know. I wanted peace for them and if that meant death then, please, God, intervene. I recently had a friend tell me that he had given two parents Narcan, a prescription medicine that blocks the effects of opioids and reverses an overdose, in case they needed it for their son. They ended up giving it back to my friend, saying that they'd had enough and what will be will be. It is a vicious cycle and those who love the addicts are all helpless.

"My family was tired both physically and mentally and my brothers just compounded the never-ending drama. You would have thought losing a brother to this dreadful drug was enough for them to see the light, but that was far from the truth. The only thing that can help a heroin addict is him. All the crying, begging, screaming, or even treatment for that matter will not work unless a person is committed to recovery. Everyone has a different rock bottom and many will never get it."

Today, Charlie and Joseph are good for months and then often relapse. Nancy is pleased that they now experience longer stretches before relapses and that when they do relapse, they are able pick up the pieces faster than in the past. "Point being, I believe they have chipped but do not go on full-blown escapades," Nancy says. "They hate it and love it at the same time."

Flo had told her daughter not to put up with what she personally had endured. But it was after Flo died that Nancy had to follow her advice. Although she still will help her brothers, there have been many times when she has made them leave her home, which she believes is what has made them strive more to stay clean.

"I hate heroin so bad and the hold it has on them," Nancy says. "I cannot believe that the very people who pollute the streets might have children of their own and have no regard for others. I was not going to endure any more pain from this drug and that is when I said enough. So around ten years ago, I tried a different approach and would say things like, 'Why do hate yourself so much? Do you like handing your whole paycheck to your pusher? Do you think they like you? They're laughing at you all. They're sitting home while you work to support a habit.' We started talking more about it, and they realized how much they hated their addiction."

Nancy admits, sadly but honestly, that she would not be surprised if, despite her brothers' valiant attempts to stay clean, she could lose them both to drug overdoses. It is a thought that breaks her heart, but one never far from her mind. She knows only too well how cunning addicts are. That the drug they seek is so powerful that people, like her brothers, literally die to get it. "But you get really sick and tired of worrying all the time," she says. "So I force myself to accept that whatever will be, will be. I must enjoy my own life and deal with whatever comes my way. I shall, no matter what, enjoy my journey."

At one point, however, wrought with grief for herself

and her mother, Nancy asked her therapist why she wasn't an addict herself, especially after all she had to endure with her family's tragedies. Her therapist told her she might have an addictive personality, but she doesn't go near any drugs because she has a complete understanding of the ramifications of addiction. All Nancy knows for sure is that she has seen way too much of the harm heroin can cause, how it can destroy a person. "Never mind my own family," she says. "I have seen girls walking in the streets, prostituting themselves because of it."

Yet, Nancy believes her main reasoning for staying away from drugs was her mother. How could she ever put Flo through the pain and suffering of having yet another child on drugs? "My father was an alcoholic, Karen's boyfriend was a drinker and on legal medication, Mark was on drugs, and, of course, Michael," she says. "Because of drugs of some sort, all of them, except for my father, were incarcerated. Point being, if you took drugs, including alcohol, out of the equation, these tragedies might not have happened. I like life. Why would I only want to coexist?"

When Flo's health began to fade, it had become impossible for Nancy to ignore the fact that her beloved mother was dying. Her mother battled breast cancer, voice box cancer, and skin cancer. In addition, she was a diabetic. But nothing was more severe than her blood condition. Flo received more than 100 blood transfusions, and according to Nancy, was literally bleeding to death. With all these hospitalizations, Nancy found much time for the two of them to talk, discussions that Nancy cherished, learning many things about her parents she might never have known. During one of these hospital stays, Flo's mother received a portacath which resulted in an infection. Her body went septic, and she did not have the strength to fight this infection. "My mother was surrounded by her family when she was called home to her final resting place, and I hope she has found the peace she so truly deserves," Nancy says. "Heaven is a better place with Flo there."

No matter how relieved she was that her mother was no longer suffering, Nancy was still devastated when Flo died. "For the first time in my life I had to deal with my family issues without her," Nancy says. "I could call my sister, which I still do, but there is nothing like your mother."

As time passed, Nancy found the pain was lessening and life went back to a new normal. One day, her twenty-year-old niece Melissa, Joseph's daughter with whom Nancy has always been very close, told her she was pregnant. While Nancy was far from thrilled at the news, she remembered her father saying there were always worse things than a girl coming home and telling you she is pregnant. "On November 10th, 2011, the Marine Corps birthday, I might add, Melissa had a beautiful baby boy she named Braylon," Nancy says.

After the baby was born, Melissa lived with her mother, and eventually the family talked about her venturing on her own. They decided that Braintree would be a good place for Melissa, since Nancy lived in nearby Dorchester, Melissa's mother in Weymouth, and the Braintree school system was good. Convinced that Melissa had a strong support system set up for herself, Nancy purchased a two-bedroom condo, into which her niece moved on May 1, 2012.

Kevin, her boyfriend and Braylon's father, moved in with Melissa in June. Things appeared to going all right when Nancy received a call from her niece on August 23rd at 12:30 in the afternoon. Barely able to make out what Melissa was saying, Nancy finally understood that Kevin had hanged himself in the condo. "It was like reliving my father's death again, minus me finding him," Nancy says. "Cops, ambulance drivers, and people were everywhere. And then I saw my niece. She was in shock, sitting on the lawn. She kept on saying, 'I tried to save him, I tried to save him.'"

When she'd walked into the condo with her son, the two of them had called out for Kevin, but there had been no answer. Braylon had wandered into the bedroom and was just standing there. Following him into the room, Melissa found Kevin in the closet. She could not believe what was happening. In a state of shock and two months pregnant with her second child, Melissa sliced her hand open while trying to cut the curtain off of Kevin's neck.

"When Melissa contacted Kevin's family to let them know the horrific news, some of them blamed her," Nancy says. "Kevin's brother told her she was not welcomed at the wake."

Nancy and the rest of Melissa's family were all mortified. "We were taking Melissa to a support group to cope and she was getting these hideous emails," Nancy says.

"I sent the brother off an email and told him to back off. One of Kevin's female cousins jumped on the bandwagon sending stuff off to Melissa. I was in a complete rage. I wanted to hurt them so bad."

Nancy could not bear to let her niece's last recollection of Kevin being that of cutting him down, so she called the mortician to see if Melissa could go to the wake privately. When he notified the family of the request, Nancy talked to Kevin's mother. His mother had been unaware of what was happening regarding the mortician, and immediately gave her blessing for such a visit. Still, Nancy's emotions remained so out of control that she could not sleep or stop crying or rid herself of the anger of wanting to physically hurt everyone who was hurting Melissa. Frightened by her rage, Nancy called her primary care doctor who ultimately diagnosed her yet again with PTSD. "But the feelings that were resurrected were like nothing I ever felt before," Nancy says. "It was pure and utter fury. It was as if my mind had been filled with emotions that had been hermetically sealed, and the lid finally popped."

Nancy thought about her mother and how she would have handled this, heartsick that her mother wasn't here for the family. She thought about Jackie and wondered if he'd felt a similar rage the night he'd killed her sister Karen. She thought of how different life would have been if her father were here. She cried for her niece who had no idea what was in store for her and for her poor little grand-nephew, just one year old. What impact would this have on him? "I was angry at God for having two more generations violated by tragedy," Nancy says. "I was so angry and knew I needed help. And thank heavens I got it."

Nancy remembers many important conversations she had with her mother, but one in particular brings her much solace. One day, in the hospital, Nancy had said, "You know, Ma, they say adversity adds character," and Flo had answered, "I disagree. I believe it reveals character." That comment reinforced Nancy's adoration and respect for her mother. "She was and is my hero," Nancy says. "If I can be half the woman she was, I will count my blessings. She taught me some of the most valuable lessons through the hardest times in her life. Even when she purchased the headstone for my sister and father, she put on it, 'Life isn't forever, love is.' I love my mother as much today as I did as if she were alive for all the things she represented to me. Imagine three heroin addict sons, one succumbing to his addiction, a daughter murdered, a husband hanged. How much she must have worried about all of us. Yet, she carried on, her head held high. She loved living. She never felt the slightest bit of shame for what had happened to her family. I often wondered how she got her strength."

When Nancy reflects on the lives of her family, she thinks about how different her parents were. While her father chose not to live for whatever his reasons were, her mother strived to survive amongst great adversity, both in her health and in regard to her children. "She knew we were not perfect, far from it, but her undying love for each one of us was always felt," Nancy says. "Over and over, she taught us to walk with our heads high and, most important, she showed and taught me that anything is reachable with persistent and hard work. She always said, 'Do not give up. There are others a lot worse off. Embrace life and reach for the stars. They are within reach.'"

Nancy does not mean, in any way, for her family's story to be a sad one because there were so many fun and memorable times in their lives. And still are.

"It is simply our history with its many twists and turns," she says. "I will not pretend that it was ordinary but, nonetheless, it was and is ours. We have our dysfunction, but so do many other families."

Today, heading to Story Land in New Hampshire with Melissa and her three adorable children or just spending time with them at a playground in Southie, Nancy is proud of the way Melissa has managed to build a new life for herself and her children.   "I have a wonderful life," Nancy says. "I have so much to be grateful for. And I am. I am totally self-sufficient today. And I grew up in a wonderful neighborhood, the best one anyone could ever want. I maintain great friendships with so many friends from South Boston, many of who are very successful and have flourished in our community. Southie was, and I believe still is, a great place to live. Yes, you have some families that have had more than their share of trials and tribulations while other families, for whatever the reason, have been spared. And I say good for them. Yes, I have had terrible losses, loved ones I will never stop loving or missing. But, oh, my, how deeply I have been blessed."

For Nancy, the greatest blessing will always be her mother. "I honestly do not know where I would be without her guidance and never ending advice," Nancy says. "I only hope that others who find themselves in the depths of despair will hear my mother's message to live for today, that it is a gift and that is why it is called the present. She knew, as did I, that there is not always tomorrow. But most of all, she always reminded us to be proud of where we came from, never ever to be ashamed. And we never were."

AFTERWORD

BY SHARON L. BAKER, PHD

When we look back on our childhoods and tell our stories, we create just that—stories. Our experiences coupled with our memories and perspectives on our past create a narrative that is part fact and part fiction, based on often biased recollections of what and whom have been most critical in shaping who we are today. These stories are often passed down from generation to generation as fact rather than fiction, as witnessed in the stories of the women of Southie.

One has to look at the stories as a whole, to recognize that all of these women use the term "Southie" to evoke something larger than life—a unique physical place, a culture with a clearly defined set of norms and expectations, an identity, and a state of mind. I think one has to go back to the beginning to make sense of this, to understand not only the dire circumstances of the Irish immigrants who settled in Southie, but also the impact that those circumstances had on their world view and their state of mind.

The potato famine was the culmination of several centuries of oppression by the British. The families who got

out were not just looking for a better life, they were flee-
ing catastrophic and traumatic losses brought about by
starvation. And they weren't embraced upon arrival, nor
for decades afterward. So their world view was shaped
by political and social oppression and death on a large
scale, and, as a result, a strong sense of betrayal and mistrust of outsiders. The narrative of this transplanted and
geographically isolated community solidified around the
belief that threats from the outside world would almost
universally be worse than anything that could possibly
happen within the community. This was a logical and
rational conclusion derived from the harrowing circumstances they had fled.

In my 30 years of practice as a psychologist, I have
worked with hundreds of trauma survivors who have
shared their histories with me in the hope of better
understanding how they have come to be who they are
today. The task of therapy is to help make sense of each
personal narrative, which starts by acknowledging their
suffering so as to make room for hope and the possibility
of healing. After listening to hundreds of stories, each one
recognizably unique in its details, I have come to understand that what is universal in the search for hope and
healing is the need to make sense out of the past in order
to create a more sensible life in the future.

The unique stories we have just read about such very
different women are uncannily consistent with regard to
the way they describe the forces that shaped their lives—
family, church, school, community, friendships, loyalty
and pride—and distill them down to a single word,

Southie. It is notable how positively each woman views her Southie upbringing, how special and privileged it still seems after decades. To someone like me, their unquestioning reverence is questionable, and, to outsiders, the norms for acceptable behavior read like a secret code that translates to significant problems. Men drank, fought, and engaged in illegal activities that often landed them in prison. Mothers regularly beat their children to discipline them. Families kept their problems secret and even within the home problems were not talked about. To survive one had to know how to take a beating and fight back.

All of this seems to contradict the notion that growing up in Southie was a wonderful experience. But these women, despite all the trauma and dysfunction that characterized life within the community, are unflagging in the pride and love they feel for it. We have to remember that these are the women who were able to survive and even thrive despite multiple traumas. Many of their friends, neighbors and loved ones were less fortunate, succumbing to addiction, suicide, and even murder.

This contradiction represents an enigma that can't be solved by looking at any one story, and is reliant on the history of Southie, its settlers, and its past trauma. The narrative is not of one woman, but of an entire people. When Southie's unique culture was uprooted by the intrusion of the outside world, it was felt as a tremendous loss. These women speak about Southie as if she were a deceased mother, gone forever, with some maternal parts not ever to be missed and others never to be recovered.

Distortions of memory are common in trauma

survivors. People who have been through traumatic experiences understandably develop beliefs that may be inaccurate but seem to serve the function of protecting them from repeating the trauma. While these beliefs may succeed in offering some measure of protection, they generally become so extreme and rigid that begin to exact a cost, and the cost is a gradual narrowing of existence through fear, mistrust, and isolation. This can happen not only to individuals but to entire communities. To us, these beliefs may appear to be at odds with current reality, but to the survivors of trauma, they seem altogether true. As a result of their distortions, trauma survivors continue to respond in the present as if it were the past, which generally isn't the most effective way to deal with life's new challenges. The work of the therapist is to challenge these rigid beliefs in order to open up life to new possibilities.

The stories the women so bravely shared in this book involving addiction, violence, and secrecy arise from a set of beliefs and norms that perpetuated trauma rather than protecting them from it. Start with the belief that abuse, whether by parents, partners, priests or nuns, is somehow a normal and expectable part of life. Adding that loyalty to family or community may come at the expense of protecting oneself. Finish off with the belief that although the people and institutions charged with protecting people may actually harm them, this is acceptable because if they weren't there, what would come at you from the outside would be far worse.

The belief that these social norms were necessary to preserve a way of life that was ultimately better and safer than what lay outside of Southie served to perpetuate them. It was a world unto itself into which the residents of Southie were born, came of age, married and had children, and continued to repeat certain patterns generation after generation. It felt safe because, despite the suffering, everyone knew the rules as well as the players, with the understanding that even if they had harsh ways of demonstrating it, people cared about other people and had their backs. That outsiders would never be so loyal was probably an accurate assessment.

The problem for trauma survivors is that the more successful they are at protecting themselves from the past, the less well prepared they are to confront the future. If change had been introduced gradually, the people of Southie might have been able to adapt, to shed their distrust bit by bit, and discover that some of their beliefs about the rest of the world were unfounded, which might in turn have decreased some of the pressure to adhere to dysfunctional social norms. Unfortunately, the busing crisis had the opposite impact, reinforcing fears and compounding a sense of betrayal. No one took notice, let alone seemed to care, that for the residents of Southie it wasn't simply about the politics of race that were at the forefront for everyone else at that time. It was about shattering an entire way of life in which a day's journey to and from school involved walking a block or two, not riding a bus across town.

This rupturing of the insularity of the Southie community served as confirmation that generations of mistrust of outside forces and fear of betrayal were, in fact, well founded. All of the women in the book look fondly, almost reverently, on the world that was Southie before it was invaded by outsiders. And despite how the rest of the world might judge things, most believe that it was a better place when Whitey Bulger and his people were there to protect them from the outside world.

After reading the stories of these six women, I am left with no doubt about their resilience or where it came from. It was passed down through each generation by the mothers who gave birth to them and raised them. By all accounts these were fearsome women whose task was to bring order to large and unruly households. With unflinching determination, using any means necessary, they pursued their mission to keep not just their families but the entire community together. They showed their love through endless hours of hard work, often working outside the home but still finding time to make the meals, polish the shoes, starch and iron the school uniforms and take care of neighbors in need. They also showed it through harsh discipline. The image of Elaine's mother lifting up a heavy bed frame to get at her daughter so she could beat her for a poor report card brings to mind a kind of maternal Hercules with the strength to carry the entire world on her shoulders. By the telling, these actions arose from—and were justified by—a singularity of purpose: to transmit the values of the family and the community to the next generation.

And it worked, as these women are nostalgic for their larger-than-life Southie childhoods, and see it as the one place they would always want to return to. This nostalgia evokes a child's view of a world that begins and ends with her mother. She is powerful, all-encompassing, and all things good and bad flow from this cord and are transmitted through the generations, passed down from mothers to daughters. But while they may say they don't want things to change, there is evidence that this is not true. They are not interested in passing on corporal punishment or pressure to stay in relationships with abusers.

Perhaps what each of these women has tried to do is to hold on to those parts of their Southie upbringing that made them strong—a sense of place, of belonging, of knowing who you are. We know that a sense of connection to others acts as a buffer when trauma occurs. While all of these women at one time or another kept certain secrets about addiction or abuse, none of them ever describe feeling completely alone and isolated. When life in Southie was harsh and cruel, some parts of her were always there, like the good mother, to remind you that you would never be alone. This may be a key to why Southie is remembered so fondly despite its many dysfunctional aspects. The certainty of being a part of something larger than oneself, larger than life itself, may have provided the necessary buffer in the face of so much trauma, fostering a resiliency in these women that allowed them to break the cycle of trauma and spawn a new generation that is more open and better able to survive and thrive in the outside world. Perhaps by holding on to the best of their Southie roots and leaving the rest behind they are freeing their own children to create a more realistic narrative about how they came to be who they are and who they are yet to become.

Dr. Baker is the Clinical Director, Women's Integrated Treatment & Recovery Program, an affiliate of the National Center for PTSD, Boston VA Medical Center

ABOUT THE AUTHOR

Phyllis Karas has been a *New York Times* best-selling author, professor of journalism at Boston University and a stringer for *People Magazine*. She has written ten books: *Brutal* was a NYT bestseller; *The Onassis Women* was the subject of a *Dateline NBC* special. Some of her other works include *Street Soldier: My Life as an Enforcer for Whitey Bulger and the Boston Irish Mob, Hunted Down: The FBI's Pursuit and Capture of Whitey Bulger,* and *An Actor and a Gentleman* (Academy Award winner Louis Gossett, Jr.'s memoir), along with four young adult novels. Her work has appeared in *Vogue, Miami Herald, Boston Magazine,* and *Moment Magazine.* She has been interviewed on C-SPAN, Hardball with Chris Matthews, CNN, Extra, and Hollywood Access

Phyllis Karas is married to Jack Karas, a pulmonary physician, and is the mother of their two sons and the grandmother of three. She lives with her husband in Massachusetts and balances her professional writing and teaching careers with her love of family, travel, and sports.

PRAISE FOR *WOMEN OF SOUTHIE*

"In *Women of Southie*, Phyllis Karas gives us compelling portraits of six enduring, vibrant women who have made it through the worst that life can throw at them—physical abuse, addiction, and post-traumatic stress disorder. Yet their intense family love and loyalty carried them through whatever was going on around them. Everyone knew the neighborhood that was ruled by legendary crime boss Whitey Bulger wasn't your white picket fence suburbia. There were drugs, an epic war between rival gangs, and more than a few murders. But most didn't know that behind this façade, even stronger women lived and loved and overcame and made their own families rocks of stability. They hold little back in telling their stories and Phyllis Karas lets us see the world through their eyes in vivid detail. Their strength and resilience are amazing, making the book a real page-turner. You won't soon forget these women who never stopped loving their town of Southie."

—CARYL RIVERS, AUTHOR OF THE BESTSELLING NOVEL *VIRGINS*

"This powerful book reads like something out of Hollywood—colorful, passionate—but in this case, all too real. Women of Southie pierces the stereotypes of working class women, telling their stories through the eyes of the women themselves. Karas and Weeks pull no punches in their unblinking portrait of Southie women, who at one turn make savagely poor decisions and, on the other, reveal deep reserves of compassion and grit. It is the story of despair, struggle, and resilience. Not to be missed."

—JUDY STOIA, EXECUTIVE PRODUCER,
PUBLIC AND COMMERCIAL BROADCASTING